Rockin' THE Blues

The Best American and British Blues-Rock Guitarists: 1963-1973

by
Dave
Rubin

Cover photos (counter-clockwise from left): Duane Allman by Joe Sia/Star File, Jimmy Page by Robert Knight, Keith Richards by Robert Knight, Roy Buchanan provided by Star File, Eric Clapton by Robert Knight

ISBN 0-634-01493-5

HAL•LEONARD® CORPORATION

7777 W. BLUEMOUND RD. P.O. BOX 13819 MILWAUKEE, WI 53213

Visit Hal Leonard Online at
www.halleonard.com

DEDICATION

I would like to dedicate this book to my daughter Michelle and my wife Cheryl, without whom I would have the blues all the time.

ACKNOWLEDGMENTS

I would like to thank the following for their support and encouragement: Ira Bolterman, Darrell Bridges, John Cerullo, Nick Koukotas, Eric Leblanc, Mike Mueller, Jeff Schroedl, Jim Schustedt, Zeke Shein, John Stix, Olav Torvund, and Brad Wendkos.

TABLE OF CONTENTS

INTRODUCTION
ROCKIN' THE BLUES: From the U.S. to the U.K.

The history of the blues is laced with irony. The national tragedy of the transatlantic slave trade begun in the 1600s sought to deprive Africans of their culture, but inadvertently exposed them to European musical traditions and instruments that led to the birth of the blues in the American south circa 1890. Some in the Anglo population had their ears open early on as evidenced by a white man, Arthur Seals, beating W.C. Handy to the distinction by just two months with the first published blues, "Baby Seals' Blues" in 1912. After "Crazy Blues" by Mamie Smith was recorded in 1920 there began a lengthy period of the blues as an integral component in the African-American community until it was superseded by soul music in the early 1960s. Throughout this entire period of time most, though certainly not all, white listeners in America applied basically benign neglect to the blues.

By the early 1950s, however, white country musicians in the South began incorporating blues licks and phrasing into a new, embryonic form of music as yet unnamed. Often they learned directly from their black neighbors or family employees out in the sticks. Merle Travis, Chet Atkins, and Scotty Moore were some of the earliest and most prominent, with Moore applying his seamless blending of country and blues licks to the music of an ambitious young man in the summer of 1954. The greasy, astoundingly charismatic singer Elvis Presley was joined by Moore and upright, "doghouse" bassist Bill Black at Sun Studios in Memphis, and their revolutionary hybrid of hillbilly boogie and blues would eventually come to be called rockabilly a few years later. In fact, it was the official, if not absolute, beginning of rock 'n' roll as a style of music and as an unprecedented youth movement. Other white cats like Carl Perkins, Jerry Lee Lewis, Dale Hawkins (whose 1957 recording of "Suzie-Q" featured James Burton's seminal blues-rock licks), Roy Orbison, and even Johnny Cash would build on Presley's success. Meanwhile, Chuck Berry was concurrently combining blues with country and western music and swing jazz (by way of jive-talking shuffler Louis Jordan) to create a distinct style that rocked *and swung*, and his influence on rock is inestimable. In addition, the chugging boogie blues of Jimmy Reed would also exert a considerable effect on both future American and English blues-rockers.

It took some time for the I–IV–V progressions of 1950s rock 'n' roll to give way to a new form of rocked up blues in the early 1960s. Roy Buchanan in the Washington, D.C. area, Robbie Robertson in Toronto, and Lonnie Mack in Cincinnati, to name three of the most prominent, began bringing an edge and energy to their version of the blues rarely found outside of black blues guitarists like Lafayette "Thing" Thomas and Auburn "Pat" Hare. Keenly aware of the potential contained in the right combination of axe and amp, they were the sonic pioneers who would fry their vacuum tubes in order to achieve the thick, overloaded sound that would thrill fans and fellow musicians alike. The blues-based San Francisco bands like Big Brother and the Holding Company, Creedence Clearwater Revival, Quicksilver Messenger Service, the Steve Miller Band, and the early Santana band that arose in the mid-1960s (and contributed so much to the music of the counterculture movement in the latter part of the decade) also understood that the "medium (loud, distorted guitars) was the message." Technology played a significant part because as the amps got bigger, so did the sound, and savvy guitarists got hip to the fact that they could riff and solo with the expressiveness and power that had previously been the domain of honking tenor saxophonists. Perhaps no one delivered this powerful, earth-shaking message better than Jimi Hendrix, at once a true bluesman and blues-rock icon.

The Allman Brothers Band with dual axemen Duane Allman and Dicky Betts were arguably the most important American group to bring all the elements together in an accessible style also steeped in authentic blues roots. Still at it after thirty-five years, they spawned a new genre known as Southern Rock that was, in fact, blues-rock with a Dixie accent. Lynyrd Skynyrd, the Marshall Tucker Band, .38 Special, the Charlie Daniels Band, Black Oak Arkansas, the Atlanta Rhythm Section, Molly Hatchet, and the Outlaws (featuring three lead guitarists like Skynyrd) all put their individual stamp on the music. Further west in Texas, Johnny Winter (like his buddy Hendrix, a blues and blues-rock monster), the Sir Douglas Quintet, the obscure Bugs Henderson, and especially ZZ Top in the 1970s purveyed their own brand of blues-rock that tended to be funkier and more low-down. On the East Coast, Mountain, with gargantuan Leslie West, raided the cultural banks of America and England for a blistering guitar attack, while Rick Derringer, a Johnny Winter band alumnus, veered between heavy blues-rock and teenage pop.

By the 1980s MTV had effectively crushed the genre as long, stringy hair, beer bellies (in some cases) and cowboy clothes did not appeal to the demographic that the cable music station was courting, though Z.Z. Top was able to adapt in spectacular "fashion" (pun intended!). The ascendance of Stevie Ray Vaughan in 1983 did not exactly resuscitate blues-rock, though he certainly gave the blues a hot shot in the arm while inspiring way too many imitators. The ironclad grip that the media giants now hold on the airwaves is almost a guarantee that classic blues-rock as now played by the young buck Joe Bonamassa will never make a substantial comeback, though the surprising success of the White Stripes is encouraging.

All Dressed Up Like A Union Jack

Across the big pond a musical revolution arose in the late 1950s that would likewise have a profound effect on guitar rock. Young English musicians were becoming enthralled with American folk music and the blues in particular. Big Bill Broonzy, Sonny Terry, Brownie McGhee, and most significantly Muddy Waters had made trips to the British Isles. Race was hardly an issue in this whitest of homogenous societies where blacks were considered exotic, noble primitives at worst. Muddy's sojourn in 1958 was especially cataclysmic. With blues piano legend Otis Spann in tow and backed by the local Chris Barber Jazz Band, Muddy's loud, keening electric slide outraged the staid British press who considered amplified blues or jazz "impure." In contrast, nascent fans like Eric Burdon and drummer John Steel who attended a show in Newcastle had their lives changed and went on to form the Animals. Though the response was overwhelmingly positive, Muddy was taken aback by the intense revulsion of some, and when he returned on a 1963 tour he performed solo on acoustic guitar. He was hardly prepared for the reaction when rabid fans that had been devouring his smoldering electric Chess sides from the 1950s wanted to know where his amp was. To his surprise, a small but hardy group of English blues musicians had sprung up in a matter of years, "playing louder than we ever played," exclaimed a perplexed Hoochie Coochie man.

Ever since Lonnie Donegan recorded Leadbelly's "Rock Island Line" in 1954 (thereby giving rise to "skiffle," a combination of acoustic country music and blues), interest in American roots music had been growing. Raucous rock 'n' rollers such as Little Richard, Jerry Lee Lewis, Fats Domino, and Chuck Berry were also influential, especially to the rockers who went on the spearhead the coming British Invasion of 1964. When records by Howlin' Wolf, Little Walter, and Bo Diddley, among others, were released in England it only expanded an already significant number of blues disciples who were bent on accurately recreating the classic sounds they revered. Alexis Korner's Blues Incorporated along with Cyril Davies and His R&B All Stars were two of the earliest and best proponents of traditional amplified country and Chicago-style blues. T.S. McPhee and the Groundhogs, the Climax Blues Band with Peter Haycock, and Chicken Shack (featuring future Fleetwood Mac singer/keyboardist Christine Perfect) with Stan Webb contained under-appreciated guitarists.

The tougher and grittier Graham Bond Organization (with Jack Bruce on bass and Ginger Baker on drums) and the Spencer Davis Group (with a teenage Stevie Winwood) though, signaled the rumblings of a new style of music best exemplified by the Yardbirds. Along with the Rolling Stones (and their blues fanatic Brian Jones), though in a more improvisational manner, they began revving up the blues beyond what had been previously imagined and were clearly the predecessors of Cream and Led Zeppelin. Playing not just faster but louder with the guitar way to the fore, they were in the vanguard of the biggest blues irony of all. Their groundbreaking versions of "I'm A Man" and "The Train Kept A-Rollin'" with Jeff Beck sent a rocked-out, highly exciting, accessible form of the blues back to American audiences. The response was as immediate and enthusiastic as raw, visceral blues always receives. In addition, with Eric Clapton, Jeff Beck, and then Jimmy Page succeeding each other in the Yardbirds, the concept of the "guitar hero" was established. Fans and aspiring guitarists looking past their pop recordings like "For Your Love" were treated to "B" sides and imported albums such as "New York City Blues," *Five Live Yardbirds*, and *Sonny Boy Williamson & the Yardbirds*. What happened then was equally unexpected and unprecedented. Determined listeners in the U.S. started discovering the original artists, often surprised that not only were many of them still alive and well but performing in their own backyard. B.B., Albert, and Freddie King, along with Otis Rush and Buddy Guy were idolized. Over the years Savoy Brown (whose members would go on to form Foghat in the 1970s) with guitarist Kim Simmonds, Ten Years After with Alvin Lee, early Jethro Tull with Mick Abrams, and Rory Gallagher and Gary Moore after leaving Thin Lizzy, would carry on the British blues tradition.

Two other related groups had the biggest impact on British and, by extension, American blues-rock. Fleetwood Mac, named for drummer Mick Fleetwood and bassist John McVie, eventually featured a triple guitar attack of Danny Kirwan, Elmore James acolyte Jeremy Spencer, and the amazing Peter Green and played exceedingly authentic blues years before they changed personnel and became pop superstars in the late 1970s. When the "Mac" formed officially in 1967, McVie, Fleetwood, and Green were veterans of John Mayall's Bluesbreakers. Mayall, affectionately known as the "Father of British Blues" for his tireless promotion of the genre since the early 1960s, had commanded the most productive and influential combo of all. Not unlike the Yardbirds, his Bluesbreakers from 1966 on "graduated" future guitar legends Eric Clapton, Peter Green, and Mick Taylor. Far from being merely a clearinghouse for spectacular string benders, however, Mayall's bands brought the music of more obscure bluesmen like J.B. Lenoir to the fore, and his experiments with acoustic instruments and jazz were prophetic.

In the 1970s Clapton pursued his solo career first with Derek & the Dominoes and then with various backing bands, mixing blues, blues-rock, and pop on his numerous albums in an approach that he still practices today. The Rolling Stones, with Mick Taylor succeeding Brian Jones, followed by Ron Wood taking over the lead guitar chair, commanded the world's stage along with Led Zeppelin and their brilliantly creative Jimmy Page. While the Stones were seeking the hit record born of the moment when blues and rock collided, the Zep was a showcase for Page's bluesy lead guitar virtuosity, as well as his eclectic compositional talents. Also making his presence felt was Robin Trower, late of Procul Harum, who debuted with a blend of Hendrix and the blues in a heady stew that flew in the face of the sensitive singer/songwriter era. Foghat, with slide-meister Rod Price and leather-lunged "Lonesome" Dave Peverett, bludgeoned the blues into a rush of pure energy. Meanwhile Jeff Beck, who had been present at the British birth of blues-rock, became restless with the genre after a shaky try at a power trio with bassist Tim Bogert and drummer Carmine Appice and pitched off into jazz/rock fusion that was lyrically improvisational, but with an underpinning of solid blues feel.

The 1980s produced a new wave of "skinny tie" retro pop bands as fodder for MTV. Zeppelin crashed and burned, and Mark Knopfler was knighted to carry on with a more refined version of the tradition in his tuneful Dire Straits, though the band quickly evolved into a vehicle for his timeless narratives. Page and Plant would reunite to explore their fascination with Moroccan music, among other pursuits, but by the 1990s the Stones were the only major players still regularly rocking the blues without self-conscious irony.

Coda

Despite the condescending dismissal of the genre by terminally blasé critics and soulless record execs, classic blues-rock continues to inspire guitarists. Crunchy tone fueling soaring solos and bone-rattling riffs over driving shuffles or heartbreaking slow blues is not prone to the winds of change for lovers of music that moves their body and spirit. Instead, it is a fertile source for endless reinvention and rebirth of the blues.

John McVie Interview

John McVie, British blues bassist emeritus, started with John Mayall's Bluesbreakers forty years ago and has been the "Mac" in Fleetwood Mac for over thirty-five years. From his vantage point he was witness to the revolutionary development of the British blues scene while observing some of its legendary guitarists up close.

Do you think John Mayall and other English blues pioneers have received the proper recognition?

No, and that's been my bitch all along, more so in the U.S. rather than in the U.K. Why hasn't John received… I don't know about recognition, but maybe a "thank you." If it wasn't for John Mayall, Alexis Korner, and Cyril Davies, who did so much to support the blues, although I am sure it would have been brought to light eventually. John hasn't gotten his fair due, I don't think.

Some of that attitude seems to come from the "politics of the blues" and the "Blues Police."

You know, B.B. King could not have been more receptive of Peter Green when Fleetwood Mac opened for him on an English tour in the late sixties. Obviously, it was because Peter was a "player." And, Willie Dixon was very nice to us in Chicago when we went to Chess Records to record in 1969. Also, the guys like T-Bone Walker and Sonny Boy Williamson that we backed up as the Bluesbreakers were fine, no problem. But, when I was supposed to play with John at the opening of B.B. King's Blues Club on the West Coast [in the late 1990s – Ed.] the feeling backstage from some musicians was really uncomfortable, just dreadful. You know, like "whitey" and "English" and "what are you doing playing 'our music?'" For want of a better word, it was a "pisser." I don't know if John felt it, but talk about being "dissed!" He was supposed to go on around 10 P.M., and then it got to be like one in the morning and I don't know if he ever even got to play.

How would you describe his role in the Bluesbreakers back in the day?

For me he was more like a director or a "guider." He would say, "Listen to this and see what you think," and it might be a Willie Dixon album, "and take it from there." I can only speak for myself, but I guess he was like a teacher, but mainly on what *not* to play. But apart from that, you were pretty much left to your own devices, which was a great thing because you weren't in a rigid structure. And, if you had needed that, you wouldn't have been invited. That was one of the things that was great about John—and I'm not blowing my own trumpet here—he picked people out that he could see something in. The best example was Peter Green, who had only been playing a very, very, very short time and almost demanded an audition, and got it. And then got the job, following a rather well-known guitarist…

Yeah, rather.

Photo © 2002 Harry Goodwin/Star File

John McVie contemplating yet another new guitar player while cradling a 1960s Fender P-Bass.

[Laughs]… who had been written about on the subway walls, "God is here." *[laughs]*

The audiences back then must have been blown away to hear the Bluesbreakers.

I imagine it must be like surfing [McVie lives in California – Ed.] because we were riding this slow wave that just got bigger and bigger and bigger. In very small places up to packed houses, wherever. It was quite exciting.

Was Mayall bothered about Clapton, Green and Taylor getting so much attention?

If he was, he kept it to himself.

How did he feel about the billing of "John Mayall and the Bluesbreakers featuring Eric Clapton," for instance?

I think Eric asked for that. I'm not sure of the politics of it, but I think it was a request from Eric. I don't think John was bitter about it. I think he enjoyed it as much as whoever was out front.

He was more than just a person who brought the blues forward, however.

Like an "usher?" *[laughs]*

Yes, but he made a contribution as a blues musician in his own right.

I agree, and he is a better guitar player now than he was back then.

What was it like playing with Clapton in the Bluesbreakers?

As it grew and the papers became more and more aware of Eric and you would see pictures of "Clapton is God" written on the walls, you would go, "Oh, that's the guy in our band." It's hard to say from the inside, but it was a joy to be in the band when he'd take off.

Was he a good "team player?"

Yeah, pretty much. He definitely had his own opinions, but it was no "argy-bargy" or shout ups, or anything like that. And, he was a lot of fun, too. To me, he seemed older than his age and more mature and more experienced—certainly more than I was. Maybe it was because of his life experience. When he had something to say to me it carried more weight and I bowed to his opinions.

What was it like meeting one of your idols, Willie Dixon, when Fleetwood Mac went to Chicago?

I was sitting there in awe. I didn't speak with him much. He was pretty tight with Greeny, and Jeremy Spence sort of latched on to J.T. Brown [session tenor saxophonist who recorded with Elmore James, among others – Ed.] to try and get Elmore stories out of him. But we were just going, "That's Willie Dixon, my God." I mean, what do you say to these people, "How ya doin', Willie?" *[laughs]* We were very young and very British, I guess. There was a lot of reticence on our part.

What was the reaction of the Chicago musicians to your band?

I think they were quite surprised, but I don't know if they were amused when Greeny opened up. It was like, "Jesus Christ! Whoa!" *[laughs]*

You guys ceased to be a novelty at that point.

Yeah. That was interesting. The whole thing was like an "event" for us.

It seems that British blues guitarists "discovered" a sound that was raw, distorted, and very appealing to young, white audiences.

Yes, you're probably right there. I also remember Mike Vernon [the late veteran producer of the Bluesbreakers, Fleetwood Mac, and other English blues bands – Ed.] deliberately trying to create a "Chicago sound," especially on the bass end, that was not clean. There was definitely an attempt to "muddy" it up *[laughs]*, to use a pun.

The irony would be that as time went on, Chess was likely trying to clean up their sound.

Probably so, yeah, and maybe we crossed somewhere.

It has also been said that one of the reasons for the distorted sound was that English people were used to listening to the records on cheap phonographs that imparted a degree of muddiness to the sound, as well.

You might have a point there, yeah, I never thought of that. We just had those record changers, we didn't have the separate turntable and stereo speakers. You know, the ones with the handle on the front and you open the lid up and you had the scratchy old arm.

The Les Paul guitar was an important ingredient in the "British sound."

Yes it was. I remember Greeny trying two or three and saying, "This one is better than that one," and I would go, "Really?" Jeremy, however, was not so into equipment. I forget what he played, but one time Mick Fleetwood had to come up and turn the tuning pegs with a pair of pliers because they were so rusted.

What was the story with Jim Marshall and his shop?

When I was around twelve I lived near there. It was the "hang" after school, and we would go in to see the musicians, like Mitch Mitchell, who was a session guy there. When we started a little band—every block had one—we used to get all our gear there. Pete Townsend and John Entwistle did a lot of business there. The original Marshall's was about 20' x 10' and you couldn't move for all the gear. Jim once made a yard square bass cabinet, a cube, out of 2 1/2" block plywood with an 18" speaker that you couldn't lift. It looked beautiful and sounded all right, but there's lots of stuff today that is lighter, smaller, and sounds better.

How has your bass rig evolved?

My stuff now, I wouldn't know how to plug it together. I think it's called job security, you know, for the bass tech? I looked at the stack and went, "Jesus, how do they do it?" Because before, you would plug the amp into the speaker and the guitar into the amp—I know how to do that. But, with this stuff, I have no idea.

Are you happy with your sound?

Yeah. The ironic thing was that after all these years I finally got what I consider a perfect bass sound for me on stage...and it was our last tour [*laughs*].

After all the success you've had with Fleetwood Mac as a pop band, would you ever consider playing in a blues band again?

Absolutely. Absolutely. Absolutely. I've got my bagpipes packed by the front door waiting on the call [*laughs*]. You know, I try to listen to what's happening now and I really have a hard time with it. I'm always going back to my original stuff that I listened to like Otis Rush, all the Willie Dixon stuff, all the old Buddy Guy stuff, all the compilation albums over the years. I just can't get behind what is happening now and then I catch myself going, "Well, that's because you're old and a fuddy-duddy." But then I go, "Oh, this is silly" and I go back and listen to what pleases me. Unfortunately, they're not making any more of it.

SCALES FOR BLUES-ROCK GUITAR

Though the best guitarists in any style inevitably stamp their individual personalities on each scale, they all worked from basically the same ones. Learning them all over the fingerboard in all keys will not only give you the background you need to solo authentically, it will increase your chops for related genres as well. All the forms shown are movable to different keys. The roots are shown in white circles.

It is recommended to learn all five patterns of the most basic of rock scales, minor pentatonic, keeping in mind the five root shapes upon which they are based. There are many possible fingering patterns, but the simplest ones shown here have two notes per string in every position.

Minor Pentatonic Scale *(Key of A)*

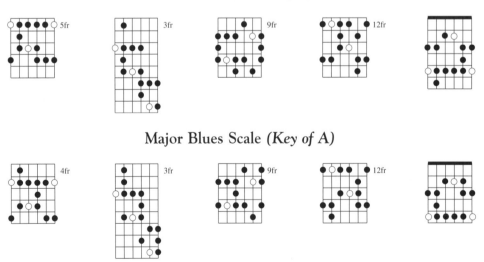

The following shapes are not presented in all five patterns, though they may be certainly learned and played that way. Instead they are optimized to facilitate bending, sliding, and other articulation devices in the way most of the giants in this book used them. Some shapes span fretboard positions and require (should I say allow) sliding or shifting between notes. Some patterns (or parts thereof) have been traditionally less-used by rock players and so are not represented here.

Basic Blues Scale *(Key of A)*

Major Blues Scale *(Key of A)*

Composite Blues Scale *(Key of A)*

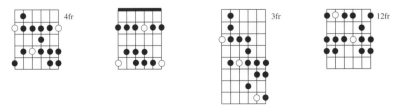

DUANE ALLMAN
Skydog

It was said that Duane Allman had an ego "as big as the Grand Canyon," but clearly he possessed the outsized talent to fill the enormous cavity. He was quoted as saying that he could be "up there" after seeing Johnny Winter at the Fillmore East in 1968, and within a year his boast was made fact. Though the Doors' Robbie Krieger had recorded slide guitar in a rock context previously on "End of the Night" in 1967, Duane's nocturnal stylings on "Dreams" from *The Allman Brothers Band* two years later brought the blues technique to the fore in popular music. Of course, it was within the context of the blues in the ABB that his impassioned playing plated his reputation as the premier bottlenecker of his generation, worthy of taking his place behind Earl Hooker, Elmore James, and Robert Nighthawk as a master of the single-string solo.

The makers of Coricidan surely never envisioned Duane Allman on an early 1960s Gibson SG soothing a "troubled mind."

Howard Duane Allman was born on November 20, 1946 in Nashville, Tennessee. Brother Gregg was born a little more than a year later on December 8, 1947, and the first of many tragedies for the Allman brothers occurred when their father was murdered in 1949 and their mother packed up the family for Florida. Gregg was lured to music first and at the age of thirteen brought home a Silvertone guitar. Duane coveted both the axe and his little brother's fledgling chops. They fought over the prize until Duane traded a trashed Harley-Davidson motorcycle for a guitar of his own. Meanwhile, he advanced at an incredible rate after Gregg showed him the I–IV–V chords in the key of E. In literally a matter of weeks Duane absorbed his brother's teachings, surpassed him, and threw himself into practicing day and night. He quit high school and urged Gregg to do the same, but the younger boy did not possess the same unshakable confidence and stayed with his studies and his plans to become a dentist.

The two Allman brothers formed a band and performed Stones, Beatles, and Yardbirds tunes up and down Daytona Beach as the Escorts and then the Allman Joys, with whom they cut versions of "Spoonful" and "Crossroads" around 1966. It was at this time that Duane fell under the spell of Cream and other heavy British blues-rockers. After Gregg graduated in 1964 he had planned to give a year to the full-time music gig that Duane desired, after which time he planned to attend college and dental school; the year stretched on a bit longer than planned. They changed their name to the Hour Glass, and their music evolved from rock to soul. With assistance and encouragement from the Nitty Gritty Dirt Band, Duane and Gregg snared a contract with Liberty Records in California, headed west, and recorded two albums. The sands quickly ran out for the Hour Glass, however, when the label nixed their idea to record a third album of blues and R&B.

While in California, Duane got sick, and Gregg did him a good turn that would have far reaching results. He bought him Taj Mahal's first album that included a cover of Blind Willie McTell's "Statesboro Blues," a version that was remarkably similar to the one that ended up on *Live At The Fillmore East*. Inspired to play slide, Duane used the Coricidan bottle that had contained his cold medicine. Gregg decided to stay in California and try his luck while Duane turned back towards home. On the way he found himself in Muscle Shoals, Alabama where he scored session work with Boz Scaggs, Otis Rush, Aretha Franklin, and Wilson Pickett in 1968. Perhaps not coincidentally, each session that his presence graced turned out to be a landmark. With Scaggs he soloed heroically on the epic version of Fenton Robinson's "Somebody Loan Me a Dime." Rush's *Mourning in the Morning*, produced by Mike Bloomfield and Nick Gravenites, was a valiant attempt to bring the legendary Chicago blues guitarist to a wider audience. Duane was there "at the creation" when he played on the Queen of Soul's "I Never Loved a Man (The Way I Love You)" and "Do Right Woman–Do Right Man" breakthrough sessions. Most significantly, however, it was his sensational work with Wilson Pickett on "Hey Jude" that set in motion forces that would change the direction of rock music. When Pickett came to Muscle Shoals at the behest of Atlantic Records to get his share of the magic emanating from Rick Hall's studio, he was presented with a different type of session guitarist from what he was used to having. Hall related the story about the fabulous mystery soloist on the revolutionary track to Atlantic Records producer extraordinaire Jerry Wexler (the man who is often credited with coining the term "Rhythm & Blues") as "Hey Jude" was becoming a million seller: "Wilson calls him Sky Man 'cause he likes to get high. He's got hair down to his butt. He's a hippie from Macon, but I'll be damned if he didn't talk Pickett into singing the song. Wilson said a Beatles tune didn't fit him. The hippie said, 'What's wrong, you don't got the balls to sing it?' That's all Pickett needed to hear." Jerry Jemmott, the amazing session bass man on the dates, also had a story to tell from the occasion: it seems that the Wicked Pickett was driving his rhythm section back to their hotel one night and Duane started to sit in the front seat. Pickett stopped him and requested that he sit in the back, saying that he did not want people (in the Southern town) to think he had "some white woman in the car with him." In time Duane's nickname evolved to "Skydog" due to his scruffy red beard. Wexler was so knocked out by Duane's melodic soulful blues, chops, and versatility that he bought his contract from Hall and put him with Delaney Bramlett, among others. In England, another white blues phenom was also mightily impressed. When he came to the States to record in 1970, Eric Clapton would ask to meet Duane and have him play on the session.

Before that in 1969, though, Duane was chafing to get his own band together, despite his success and accolades from the various Muscle Shoals sessions, and he returned to Jacksonville, Florida. A short stint in the Second Coming with Dickey Betts and Berry Oakley gave him access to a second lead guitarist and a sympathetic bassist. He added the tandem drummers Butch Trucks and Jaimoe (Johnny Lee Johnson) Johanson and convened an epochal jam. Buzzed with the possibilities, but lacking a lead singer, in March he summoned Gregg back from Los Angeles. Little brother was miserable doing grossly inappropriate material with Southern California studio pros and hitchhiked home. When he arrived at the first rehearsal he was intimidated by the power of the assembled musicians, but a run through of Muddy Waters' "Trouble No More" convinced him and everyone else in the room that Duane's dream band was ready to rock the blues. Within a week Gregg composed "Black-Hearted Woman" and "Whipping Post."

The Allman Brothers Band signed with the newly created Capricorn Records and went on the road in Florida and Georgia before ducking into the studio for their first album. The eponymous release in 1969 was not an immediate commercial success, selling less than 50,000 copies. Reviews were positive, however, and the group attracted a following that would grow. Their seamless blending of blues and rock with elements of jazz improvisation set them apart from other blues-rock outfits of the era. Gregg's raspy vocals had the ring of the real deal, and the twin lead guitar harmonies of Duane and Dickey, not heard since the heyday of Western Swing in the 1940s, gave them a readily identifiable signature sound. The band soon became known for their marathon jams in concert as Dickey fretted and Duane bottlenecked the audience into ecstasy over the mammoth groove of the muscular rhythm section that included Gregg's vibrant Hammond B-3 organ pads.

In 1970 the ABB began work in Macon, Georgia on their second offering, *Idlewild South*, with former Cream producer Tom Dowd. During the course of the sessions Eric Clapton's manager called to inform Dowd that his client wanted to come to Florida to record with his new band, Derek & the Dominoes. When Dowd relayed the news to Duane, the Allman brother asked if he could stop by to watch one of his idols in action. Then, when the Brothers were scheduled to play a gig in Miami in the summer Clapton was anxious to see the cat that had scared the wits out of him with his playing on "Hey Jude" and attended the show with Dowd. Though Duane freaked out when he saw Clapton down front, the entire band went back to Criteria Studios afterwards for an all-night jam.

When it came time for "Eric" & the Dominoes to record *Layla and Other Assorted Love Songs*, Duane was all set to watch when "Slowhand" insisted that he also play. What started out to be a "guest" appearance on a couple of tracks ended up as a full-scale collaboration on the entire album. All parties involved agreed that Duane's presence spurred Clapton (an occasional underachiever) to extend himself beyond the usual, and his contribution to the immortal title track cannot be underestimated. Duane would always consider the album some of his best playing, and few would argue that it represents some of the greatest blues and blues-rock wailing ever committed to tape. Clapton was so gassed that he invited Duane to join the Dominoes. He demurred to remain with the Brothers, but it is rumored that he did play out with the group for a number of shows.

Idlewild South showed a greater depth of material with acoustic tunes like Gregg's "Midnight Rider" and Dickey Betts' masterpiece, "In Memory of Elizabeth Reed." Out on the road the Brothers were building a reputation as a performance band without peer, stretching improvisations to thirty minutes and more. In March of 1971 they played a week at the Fillmore East in New York City that was recorded, mixed down, and released as a double album in the fall. Though rabid fans would sometimes comment that it represented the ABB on just an "average" night, it has come to be regarded as one of the greatest live albums in history. Their version of T-Bone Walker's 1947 "Stormy Monday," via Bobby Blue Bland's 1961 rendition, has become the standard against all subsequent covers are measured. The album went gold on October 15, but on October 29, twenty-four-year old Duane was killed on his Harley-Davidson Sportster XLCH chopper in Macon.

The band was about halfway through *Eat A Peach*, their third studio album, and they completed the recording with Betts finishing up the remaining guitar tracks. Duane was prominently featured on the majority of tunes, however, including "Mountain Jam" (based on Donovan's "First There is a Mountain") that covered one complete disk of the double album. Duane's pyromaniacal slide on Sonny Boy Williamson's "One Way Out" would help to make it, similar to "Stormy Monday," the benchmark for all future versions, and his "Little Martha" along with Betts' "Blue Sky" would become ABB classics. The LP became the band's first to break into the Top Ten at #5. During the course of cutting the follow up to *Eat A Peach* Berry Oakley also died in a motorcycle accident on November 12, 1972—not far from where Duane crashed. The group would continue on with one guitar and Chuck Leavell added on keyboards until Dan Toler arrived in 1978; Warren Haynes filled the second chair ten years later. They continue to roll on into the twenty-first century despite having fired Dickey Betts after thirty years of living the blues together.

Duane Allman brought a passion for the blues, fired with the energy of rock and the improvisational depth of jazz, to create a legacy on slide guitar that endures. In three short years with the Allman Brothers Band he used his guitar to eloquently speak his thoughts in a wordless, lyrical poetry.

The Blues Guitar Style of Duane Allman

Duane had the chops and the brass to back them up, but it was his soul and Southern-brewed phrasing that distinguished his blues. Black musicians like Wilson Pickett and Cornell Dupree gained great respect for him after experiencing his music first-hand at recording sessions. Late 1950s gold top and sunburst Les Pauls, along with SGs and the occasional Strat, were his main instruments.

Track 1 contains a sublime sample of his slow blues circa the *Fillmore East* era. Using the G composite blues scale (blues scale plus Mixolydian mode) in the root and extension positions for the most part, he negotiates the changes skillfully, with grace and power. Be sure to pay particular attention to the rests, which are as musical as the notes themselves, and Duane's thick-as-molasses vibrato. In measures 1 and 2 the tonality-defining major 3rd (B) is employed to establish the I chord (G). Check out the jazzy 6th (E) in measure 4 over the G13 chord (E functioning as the 6th and the 13th note). In measures 5 and 6 over the IV (C) chord, Duane makes a somewhat uncharacteristic scale change to the C composite blues scale in the root position. By restricting his note selection to the 5th (G), 3rd (E), 6th (A), and root (C), as opposed to the ♭7th (B♭), for instance, he purveys a melodic, consonant, and diatonic feeling. The heavy emphasis on the D notes in measures 7 and 8 (how cool is that F to D move on beat 1 of measure 7?) of the I chord elicit anticipation of the V chord (D) in measure 9, highlighted by the incremental bend to the D in measure 8. Observe the flurry of sixteenth notes in measure 9 that adds tension and dynamics. Duane's improvised turnaround in measures 11 and 12 outlines the I, IV, I, and V changes perfectly, nailing the root and ♭7th of each dominant tonality along the way.

TRACK 1

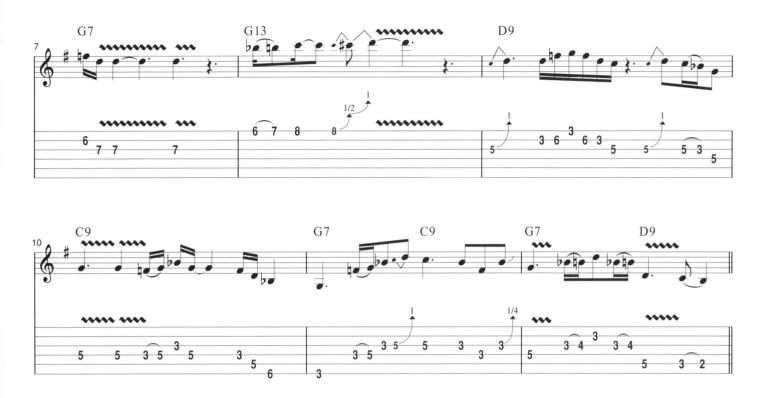

The slide-*meister* was fond of open E tuning, and Track 2 (a strutting, macho shuffle) contains a slice of his slashing bottleneck work as hot as a summer night in Atlanta. Dig how the majority of the solo is centered around the seventeenth fret, commensurate with the tonic chord (A) and similar to the way Elmore James approached soloing in open D. (Note: Open E and D are relatively the same except that the pitches go up for E instead of down for D). More about phrasing than note selection, Duane's solo still nails the critical notes to delineate the chord changes. Over the I chord (A), unsurprisingly, this mostly involves the root (A) nicked on strings 1 and 4. During the IV chord (D) changes in measures 5 and 6, he manages to cover the root (D) at fret 15 on string 2 along with the 5th (A) on string 1 at fret 17. Over the V chord (E) in measure 9 we hear an unusual ♭6th (C) in conjunction with the root (E). Likewise, measure 10 (IV chord) contains the gritty 4th (G) and jazzy 9th (E) as a tension-generator. Satisfying resolution is achieved in measures 11 and 12 of the turnaround with diligent repetition of the root (A). However, inasmuch as the turnaround maintains momentum by staying on the I chord throughout, Duane's rush up to the B (9th) and C♯ (10th) gooses the solo hard into the implied next 12-bar chorus.

Performance Tip: Duane picked with his bare right-hand fingers, as he felt that the use of picks (flat or finger) with a slide prevented a guitarist from having any direct contact with the strings. That said, he liked to wear his iconic, glass Coricidan bottle on his ring finger. This still afforded him the opportunity to play some chordal forms, particularly open position boogie patterns, though in a band with a second guitarist and a Hammond B-3 organist, he was not required to play much rhythm when sliding. It is highly recommended that all slide guitarists try to wear their slides on their pinky fingers (like the country blues cats), however, in order to allow the widest range of chord forms.

TRACK 2

Open E Tuning:
(low to high) E–B–E–G#–B–E

Moderate Shuffle ♩ = 120

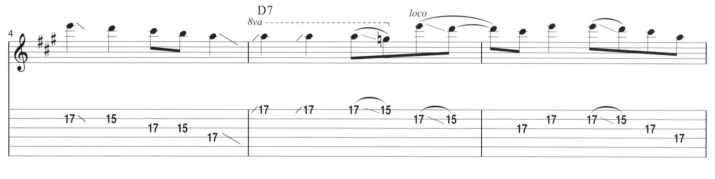

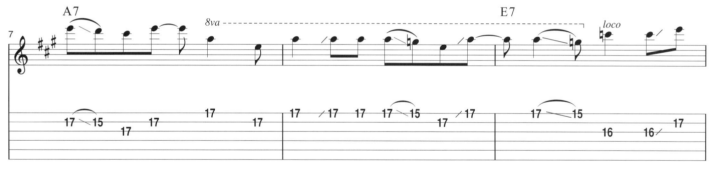

Duane Allman Selected Discography

The Allman Brothers Band (Polydor)

Idlewild South (Polydor)

Live at Fillmore East (Polydor)

Eat a Peach (Polydor)

JEFF BECK
El Becko

If Jeff Beck were a baseball player being considered for the Hall of Fame, his "numbers" would make him a shoe-in. Indeed, he could possibly accrue more votes than anyone else, including all-time MVPs like Jimi Hendrix, as a true artist with his bat (axe). Beck pioneered the artistic use of extreme volume, distortion, and feedback, not to mention Eastern-sounding modalities and "jazz" scales, with enough righteous blues feeling to have sustained a career as a first-rate bluesman. On top of that, he continues to progress and explore his possibilities on the guitar with undiminished vigor and enthusiasm, refusing to live in the past or rest on his numerous accomplishments. As his esteemed peer and former band mate Jimmy Page once said, "When he's on, Beck is probably the best there is."

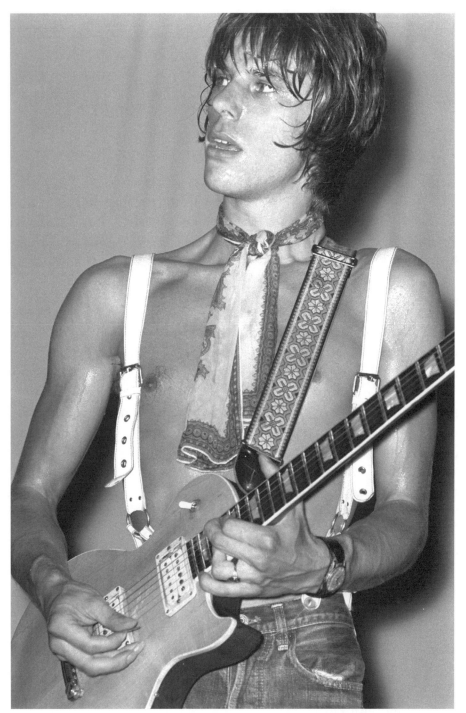

Photo by Robert Knight

The well-dressed English blues master:
Jeff Beck making mischief on a Gibson Les Paul 'Burst.

Geoffrey Arnold Beck was born on June 24, 1944 in Wellington, Surrey, England. When he was eight he began piano lessons at his parents' urging and applied himself to the tune of practicing several hours a day. Eventually he lost interest and started studying the cello and violin with an uncle, an experience that likely planted the seeds for his experiments with sustain in the early sixties. When he was 12 he entered Junior Art School, a calling that his fellow Brits like Eric Clapton, Mick Jagger, and John Lennon, among many others, also heard. His desire to play the guitar arrived simultaneously with his discovery of rockabilly music and the release of *The Girl Can't Help It* in 1957 featuring Gene Vincent with the outrageous Cliff Gallup on guitar. He built an electric guitar out of a wooden box and adapted a radio an as amp. Two years later when he was just fifteen Beck was good enough to play in the Deltones, performing covers of Hank Marvin and the Shadows as the recordings of Gallup and James Burton with Ricky Nelson provided further inspiration.

In 1960 Beck further advanced his fine arts education when he began attending Wimbledon Art School. Meanwhile, he continued to progress on the guitar as his interests broadened to include jazzers like Barney Kessel, Charlie Byrd, and especially Les Paul. Equally important to his development, the blues entered his life via B.B. King. At the same time his parents encouraged an interest in classical music, and Ravel's "Bolero" held a fascination for him that would play itself out in the recording studio years later when he cut "Beck's Bolero" in 1967 with Jimmy Page and Keith Moon. In 1961, however, his musical career was just starting to heat up as he formed a band called The Night Shift. Their first gig was at a fairground where they opened for Neil Christian & the Crusaders with Jimmy Page on guitar. Beck's sister would later make the introduction between the two future rock guitar legends.

By 1962 Beck was getting further into the blues through the hardcore Westside Chicago sound of Buddy Guy and Otis Rush. He joined the Tridents to play R&B and blues and made his first three recordings, including "Nursery Rhyme," the first hint of the bold new territory into which he was going to drag rock guitar "screaming" and "crying" in the years to come. David Bowie once commented that after seeing Beck with the Tridents at Eel Pie Island, he was never so knocked out until Stevie Ray Vaughan performed at the Montreux Jazz festival in 1982.

As Beck's reputation started to build and spread he was offered studio gigs beginning in 1963 and is reported to have experimented with feedback at this time. His flash guitar would soon catch the attention of a seminal British Invasion band that would go on to create tremendous impact under his visionary influence. Members of the Crawdaddy Club formed the Yardbirds in 1963 after being inspired by the Rolling Stones. They soon sacked guitarist Tony "Top" Topham for not being bluesy enough and snared their first future guitar god, Eric Clapton. Ever the purist, however, Mr. Slowhand found the Yardbirds heading in a direction way too pop for him and was considering splitting during the "For Your Love" sessions in early 1965. Meanwhile, Beck was surreptitiously laying down guitar tracks with the band for "Heart Full of Soul," "Steeled Blues," (featuring Beck on slide), "Still I'm Sad," and "Evil Hearted You" at Advision Studio in London. In March Clapton left to run off and join John Mayall's Bluesbreakers after contributing the boogie bass pattern to the Yardbirds smash single "For Your Love." The band apparently planned to have his considerable shoes filled by Jimmy Page, but he turned down the honor and suggested Beck—a rather obvious choice. Whatever the initial feelings of the band, they must have altered over time as Beck turned his Fender Esquire into a sonic paintbrush with fuzz, feedback, tremelo, and reverb. "Shapes of Things," "I'm a Man," and particularly "Over Under Sideways Down" were light years ahead of the Stones and Beatles, not to mention the other Invasion groups. The rest of the year was a rocket ride culminating in a U.S tour in the fall where Beck was accorded full rock star status by admiring groupies. Adding to the Yardbirds' prestige were recording sessions at Sun Studios in Memphis where they cut the rollicking "The Train Kept A-Rollin'" and "You're a Better Man Than I" and at Chess Records in Chicago where "New York City Blues," the rave up "I'm a Man," and the prophetic "Shapes of Things" hit vinyl.

1966 saw continued studio and live action, as well as the genesis of Beck's rep as being "difficult." Though he had nowhere near the guitarist's ability, lead singer/harmonicist Keith Relf jostled for the spotlight and, according to Beck, had the annoying habit of noisily using an atomizer onstage during the guitar solos. Nonetheless, in early summer rock guitar fans were bedazzled when Paul Samwell-Smith left and Jimmy Page joined the band on bass and second lead. The release of "Happenings Ten Years Time Ago" b/w "Psycho Daisies" in the fall gave only a hint of the Beck/Page possibilities, which would never reach full fruition. The band with the "dream team" on guitars appeared in new wave director Michelangelo Antonioni's *Blowup* in the fall of 1966, however, where they performed a hastily disguised version of "The Train Kept A-Rollin'" dubbed "Stroll On." The director had originally wanted The Who to perform in his swinging sixties London fantasy, and Beck had to reluctantly pull a "Townshend" by smashing a cheap Japanese guitar for the climax of the tune after playing a cool Les Paul sunburst in the previous shots. Then he was hospitalized twice for "tonsillitis" while on another U.S. tour, fueling rumors back in London that he was looking for an exit strategy in order to pursue a solo career. In December, after an amazingly productive and historic eighteen-month period, Beck quit the Yardbirds.

Hot on the trail of a vocalist to front his band, he had the first Jeff Beck Group together in early 1967 with Rod Stewart and future Rolling Stones guitarist Ronnie Wood (who would soon switch unhappily to bass). In March, Beck's first single was released containing his guitar *and vocals* on "Hi Ho Silver Lining" b/w "Beck's Bolero." The B-side instrumental featured Jimmy Page, future Led Zeppelin bassist/keyboardist John Paul Jones, and Who drummer Keith Moon and is considered a landmark that influenced, among many others, Hendrix's version of "All Along the Watchtower."

Two guitar-centric albums that were treasured by fans and fellow plectrists, *Truth* (1968) and *Beck-Ola* (1969) resulted from the uneasy collaboration with the blues diva Stewart. Though thoroughly grounded in the blues, Beck's ongoing creative use of distortion, feedback, and other effects are now seen as proto-heavy metal rumblings. Alas, though the tensions in the band produced great music, it eventually led to Stewart and Wood splitting to join the Small Faces and Beck going his own way again.

An idea for a dream power trio with former Vanilla Fudge bassist Tim Bogert and drummer Carmine Appice was kicked about, but a near-fatal car accident in 1970 sidelined "El Becko," and his plans for the group were put on ice. After Beck had recovered from his injuries in 1971 he convened another Jeff Beck Group with singer Bobby Tench and keyboardist Max Middleton as Bogert and Appice galloped off to form Cactus. The "new" Jeff Beck Group produced two uneven albums of instrumental and vocal music that nonetheless pointed the way towards his greatest post-Yardbirds triumph in the mid-1970s as he logically gravitated towards jazz. In the interim Cactus had disbanded, and Beck recklessly threw in with the overblown egos of Bogert and Appice for the ill-fated Beck, Bogert & Appice. One studio album later, the lack of original material and strong vocals, along with Bogert's propensity for playing "lead bass," led to the dissolution of BBA in 1973. R.I.P.

For nearly two years Beck lay low. In 1975, however, he released the quietly spectacular, George Martin-produced *Blow By Blow*, breaking new ground for him and improvising guitarists everywhere. A stunning selection and combination of jazz, rock, funk, and blues with the certifiable classics of Stevie Wonder's "'Cause We've Ended as Lovers" and the original "Freeway Jam," the album became a critical and commercial success. A year later he began a short but productive association with electronic keyboard wizard and Mahavishnu Orchestra member Jan Hammer and followed up with the much edgier *Wired*. Fully established as a true artiste of the electric guitar to be reckoned with, Beck set off on a tour with Hammer resulting in the exciting *Jeff Beck with the Jan Hammer Group - Live*. On top of his game and receiving long-overdue acclaim for his singular talents, he nonetheless settled into a life of seclusion for the next three years.

In 1980 he put out *There and Back* with Hammer and then sat it out for another five years. Niles Rodgers produced the pop-styled *Flash* in 1985 with a gaggle of guest vocalists, including the preening

Rod Stewart on Curtis Mayfield's gospelly "People Get Ready"—Beck's only hit single at #48—while "Escape" won a Grammy for Best Rock Instrumental. Also of significance, it was the first album that he recorded with his new, "pick-less" fingerstyle technique.

True to form, Beck "rested" for the next four years but returned in 1989 with the album that would pave the way for his future (and futuristic!) musical explorations down to the current day. *Jeff Beck's Guitar Shop with Terry Bozzio and Tony Hymas* featured the equally devastating chops of the master drummer (Zappa, Missing Persons) and keyboardist pushing Beck into grooves, riffs, rhythms, and melodies that earned the disk the Grammy for Best Instrumental Rock album. A memorable tour with Stevie Ray Vaughan followed, giving lucky fans a chance to marvel at two of the greatest electric guitarists of all time. In 1993 he revisited his youth and roots with the Big Town Playboys for *Crazy Legs*, a tribute to his rockabilly hero Cliff Gallup. A loving homage, it features unadorned, note-for-note recreations of the original guitar parts.

With his new "mates" Bozzio and Hymas, Beck has recorded *Who Else?* (1999), *You Had It Coming* (2001), and *Jeff* (2003). Each succeeding disk has found him on top of contemporary techno and dance trends with brutally intense rockers and heartbreaking ballads. In the summer of 2003, he embarked on an unprecedented tour with B.B. King, including an A&E *Live by Request* appearance and a transcendent, historic appearance at King's Manhattan club.

The Blues Guitar Style of Jeff Beck

A prodigiously talented and creative guitarist whose contribution to the electric guitar is perhaps only second to Jimi Hendrix, Jeff Beck cuts right to the heart of the real blues when dipping back into the genre. Though his contemporaries (and fellow former 'Birds) Eric Clapton and Jimmy Page are better known for having the blues as an ongoing, highly visible element of their music, Jeff can more than hold his own against his blues brothers. After starting out with a vintage Fender Esquire and then a Les Paul Black Beauty, he switched to Strats full time in the late 1970s and now has a chunky neck signature model to brandish with élan.

Jeff is a melodic scale-master with a thorough knowledge of the fingerboard, but the romping shuffle of Track 3 finds him ensconced in the basic box of the E blues scale in the twelfth position. Within those confines, however, he "honks" the blues through his guitar while marking the changes simply with the appropriate root notes. Over the I chord (E) in measures 1–4 he employs well-placed and phrased bends around regular resolution to the root (E). Measure 5 (IV chord, A) contains a "Beckism" where he bends the root (A) to the 9th (B) while holding down the 4th (D), letting both notes sustain on the edge of feedback for a measure and a half. Dig how measure 7 (I) contains a tight cluster of notes based around the B, A, and G degrees from the scale that is similar to measures 1 (I) and 10 (IV), functioning as a motif. Measures 8 (I) and 9 (V) exhibit wide intervals, another Beck characteristic that shows up in his vaunted rock work as well. The dynamic effect of this type of implied rapid ascent or descent of the scale can be quite breathtaking. Likewise, the sustaining of notes across the bar line in measures 1, 2, 3, 5 (as mentioned), and 9 also contrasts handsomely with the short, compact phrases of measures 4 and 8. Do not miss the slick implication of an A9 tonality on beat 3 of measure 11 with the B/G (9th and ♭7th) double-stop.

Performance Tip: Maintain the bend of the A (4th) to B (5th) with your ring finger in measures 2 and 3 while holding the D (♭7th) down with your pinky.

TRACK 3

Moderate Shuffle ♩ = 120 (♫ = ♩♪)

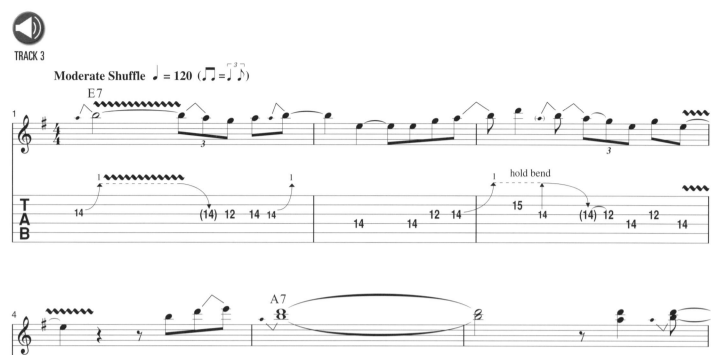

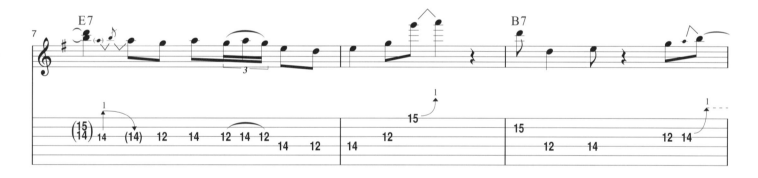

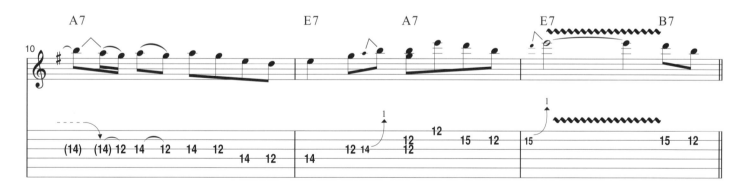

On the slow blues of Track 4 Jeff pushes the bounds a little further with a liberal selection of bends and special emphasis on some unusual scale tones for the blues. This can be clearly seen in measures 1–3 over the I chord (B) where he starts off with a jolt by playing a unison bend on the ♭7th (A) in measure 1 (repeated in measure 3) and a unison bend on the 4th (E) in measure 2. Observe how he does not give in to resolving to the root (B) even in measure 4, though he does execute a tangy double-string bend (F♯/D raised to G/E and released back down) on beat 3 that he sustains to become the 9th and ♭7th of E. In measures 5 and 6 (IV chord, E) he settles in at the 6th-string root position of the B blues scale with attention lavished on the root note (E) in measure 5, but focuses on the 5th (B) and F♯ (9th) notes in measure 6. The root note (B) is finally touched upon in measures 7 and 8 over the I chord. In measures 9 (V chord, F♯) and 10 (IV) Jeff rattles off a series of triplets involving the G♯ and B notes (functioning as the 9th and sus4th of the V and the 3rd and 5th of the IV chord, respectively). Not content to "cool it" for the turnaround, he combines the 5th (F♯ on string 1) with the C♯ (9th) bent to the D♯ (10th) in measure 11 to engender even more musical tension. Measure 12 receives no mercy, either, as Jeff highlights the C♯ (9th) over the I and the ♭7th (E) over the V chord.

Performance Tip: Pull down on the F♯/D double-stop in measure 4 with your index finger. This should automatically raise the D one step and the F♯ one-half step higher in pitch.

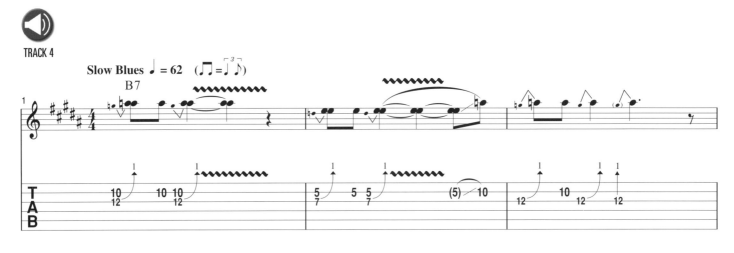

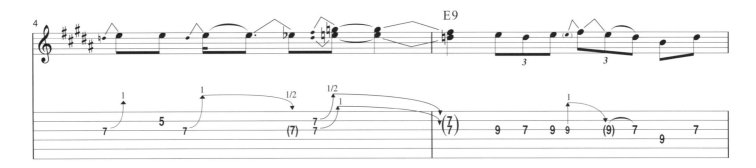

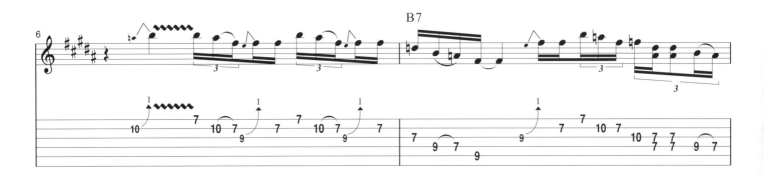

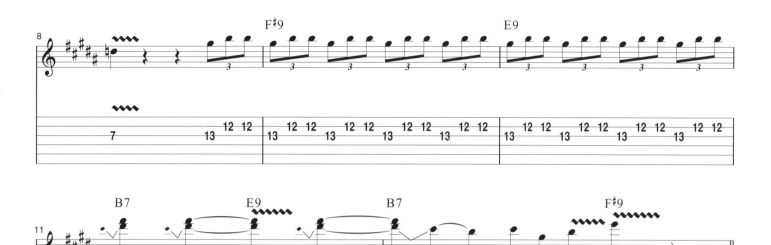

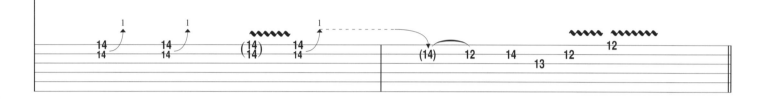

Jeff Beck Selected Discography

With the Yardbirds:

For Your Love (Epic)

Over Under Sideways Down (Epic)

Solo:

Truth (Epic)

Beck-Ola (Epic)

Blow by Blow (Epic)

Jeff Beck's Guitar Shop (Epic)

Who Else! (Epic)

ROY BUCHANAN
Roy'z Bluz

WNET, New York City's PBS TV station, made a remarkable documentary in 1971 about Roy Buchanan called *The World's Greatest Unknown Guitar Player;* tragically, the title would go on to unwittingly become his epitaph. Due to a combination of circumstances and factors, with most having to do with this complicated individual's reticent and baffling personality, his reputation would never rise much above cult status despite the fact that his stupendous technique and heartbreakingly deep expression puts him in a class by himself. Though the alto saxophone is often referred to as the instrument closest to the human voice, Buchanan could make his guitar cry with a verisimilitude unmatched in popular music history. What made it so profound was that the cry was actually emanating from deep inside his tortured soul.

Frank Driggs Collection

*Roy Buchanan caught in the act of jilting his signature Tele for a
1950s Gibson Les Paul fitted with P-90 pickups.*

Leroy Buchanan was born on September 23, 1939 in Ozark, Arkansas to Bill Buchanan and Minnie Bell Reed. In 1941 the family moved to Pixley, California where Bill, the former Depression-era sharecropper in Arkansas, became a day laborer on farms in the San Joaquin Valley. Roy was attracted to the guitar when he was five and learned a few chords on an old box until his cousin broke it. Four years later his parents bought him a Rickenbacher lap steel, and he began taking lessons with Clara Louise Presher from Bakersfield. After three years Mrs. Presher was dismayed that young Buchanan had learned all of his music by ear rather than by learning to read music as instructed. Nonetheless, she imparted the invaluable wisdom to him that what was most important of all was to play with feeling—a lesson that he clearly never forgot. In addition, the use of his right hand fingers to pick the strings on the lap steel would remain a significant element of his vaunted technique even after he began to incorporate a flat pick.

Buchanan listened to steel players on the radio, in particular the renowned Jerry Byrd with Hank Williams, whom he once described as "a really smooth player" in *Guitar Player Magazine*. He began playing at school and church functions and came to the attention of the Waw Keen Valley Boys, who brought him in to play lap steel in their band. Buchanan was just 12 years old but consistently outshone his band mates. In 1952 he bought a flat top acoustic to emulate the playing of Roy Nichols (Merle Haggard's lead man), and sometime later was exposed to the blues firsthand in Stockton, California. In high school he put a band together called the Dusty Valley Boys, which led to gigs in local joints during the rise of the Bakersfield honky tonk sound that combined blues with country and western music. At sixteen, however, playing music became his total obsession, and he quit school to go live with his brother and sister in Los Angeles. He brought a Gibson electric arch top and a Martin flat top with him, though he had already briefly owned the instrument with which he would become eternally connected—a 1953 Fender Telecaster.

An unscrupulous promoter hooked Buchanan up with drummer Spencer Dryden (later of the Jefferson Airplane and the New Riders of the Purple Sage), and they went out on the road in 1956 with the Heartbeats. Left high and dry in Oklahoma City, Buchanan hired on as the staff guitarist on the "Oklahoma Bandstand" where he would have a chance meeting with Dale Hawkins. Hawkins had recently scored a major rock 'n' roll hit with "Suzie-Q" featuring future super-picker James Burton. Buchanan was tapped to fill his shoes, and they cut a version of Little Walter's "My Babe" in 1958. For the next two years the two hit the road hard, and Buchanan learned to pop his strings as well as his pills. The two pursuits would become intertwined in his life until the end.

After his grueling apprenticeship with Hawkins, Buchanan bummed around between bands before settling in Washington, D.C. in 1960. The same year he put his estimable chops on display when he recorded two versions of "After Hours," a classic slow blues that had been a hit for Erskine Hawkins in 1940 and that Buchanan had heard Jimmy Nolen play in his blues days before he became a funk pioneer with James Brown in the mid-1960s. He got reacquainted with the Telecaster and still played the occasional gig with Dale Hawkins, and in 1961 they made a landmark foray into Canada that has become the stuff of legend in the history of rock 'n' roll. In Toronto they met up with Dale's brother Ronnie, who immediately snagged Buchanan away to play for a short while in his band, the Hawks. Not coincidentally, Ronnie also wanted him to mentor his young, undisciplined firebrand, Robbie Robertson. By this point Buchanan had developed most of his signature tricks like volume swells, detuning his bass strings while mandolin picking, bending the neck of his Tele as well as his strings, and achieving whistling, artificial harmonics. Robertson was duly impressed and would go on the with the Hawks/the Band to back Bob Dylan while making memorable, original American roots music, his stinging Tele and Strat licks always adding tasty spice to the mix. Buchanan also made recordings with the "other" Hawkins brother, Jerry, including a version of "Linda Lu" that was copied by Ray Sharpe and turned into a big hit for the Texan in 1958.

Buchanan became the dream sideman for a string of journeyman leaders in the 1960s while treating lucky club-goers to the most spectacular blues, blues-rock, country, and country rock guitar playing imaginable. He also met Danny Gatton at this time, and the two would become fast friends, if not serious competitors for top Tele-dog in the metropolitan Washington area. Buchanan's interest in Gatton's playing became such an obsession that he would call the club where Gatton was playing (if Buchanan had a conflicting gig) and have Gatton leave the phone off the hook so he would not miss a lick of the future virtuoso.

Playing along the New Jersey shore, Buchanan would come to the attention of Seymour Duncan and Les Paul, who would both tout his prowess. Playing on "Potato Peeler" by Bobby Gregg in 1962 in Philadelphia, he let loose with a pinched harmonic for likely the first time in recorded history. His status as a local legend in the Washington, D.C. area grew as other guitarists slowly spread his name by word of mouth. In 1968, however, he saw Jimi Hendrix in concert and was so disconcerted by seeing the Voodoo Child making his sounds with effects and stomp boxes that he actually *quit* playing for a while to go to barber school. Charlie Daniels contacted him around this time and brought him into the studio to record an album for Polydor, but Buchanan was greatly dissatisfied with the project that submerged his distinct talent, and it went unissued.

Back out on the local bar scene again, Buchanan finally got a band together called the Snakestretchers and recorded a primitive-sounding LP that came in a burlap bag. *The Washington Star* and the *Washington Post* wrote articles, one of which got reprinted in *Rolling Stone*, and the buzz was out. A WNET producer saw the article, went and heard Buchanan and decided to make the documentary that would make the world notice the "greatest unknown guitar player," despite Buchanan's continuing efforts to the contrary. In short order he acquired a manager and a producer at Polydor who got him back in the studio. With *Roy Buchanan* in 1972 and the modestly titled *Second Album* in early 1973, the world did get a peek at what pilgrims who had sought him out in person were raving about. The second release was especially effective, as it was mostly instrumental and contained a fair sampling of the Buchanan aesthetic that remains his studio high point. During the recording of his third LP, *That's What I'm Here For* in late 1973, Buchanan was approached by John Lennon, who was working on an album in another Polydor studio, to appear on each other's recordings but, in his typical self-destructive fashion, Buchanan turned down the offer.

More records and touring followed, and rock stars from Eric Clapton (who nicked his arrangement for "Further on up the Road" without giving credit) to Jeff Beck (who had seen the documentary, was floored, and would later dedicate his version of Stevie Wonder's "'Cause We've Ended as Lovers" to the Tele champion on his *Blow by Blow* album in 1975) began to notice. Disillusioned with the commercial response to his Polydor albums led him to Atlantic records where he would be ill-served with production and material that tried to make one of the most unique and enigmatic players on the planet into a pop star. By 1977 his career, such as it was, began to have the wheels come off as his longtime band quit after a tour of Japan in 1977 and he would turn to pickup bands for the next several years. Around 1980 Buchanan was hospitalized for severe injuries. The official story was that the police had beaten him for some infraction, but a rumor founded on strong suspicions suggests that he tried to unsuccessfully hang himself in his jail cell. In the early 1980s he was an itinerant guitar player with a cocaine habit. He even retired his 1953 Telecaster, an icon among guitarists, in favor of new Teles, Strats, and Les Pauls before settling on a custom Tele-type instrument.

Once again, however, fortune came Buchanan's way from an interested outsider when Alligator Records prexy Bruce Iglauer happened to catch a gig in Toronto in 1984. When Iglauer saw him again the same year in Chicago, a friendship and a record deal was initiated. With blues expert, writer, and DJ Dick Shurman producing, a series of excellent albums showcasing Buchanan's talent and rivaling his best work were released. The first, *When a Guitar Plays the Blues*, was even nominated for a Grammy for Blues Album of the Year.

With an updated sound and production that he liked (though Buchanan "purists" were not so sure), he went on the road with a power trio consisting of young cats on bass and drums. In 1988 he opened for the Band (minus Robbie Robertson and Richard Manuel, who had hung himself two years earlier) and just before an Australian tour he shaved his head. During a break off the road on August 14 he became involved in a domestic dispute with his wife Judy in their Fairfax, Virginia home. He stormed out and was picked up by the police and charged with public intoxication. According to police records, he was discovered in his cell with a crushed larynx and died on the way to a hospital. The official story was that he had hung himself with his shirt but many friends and family members, including his wife, believe he was the victim of brutality. Fifteen years later the questions remain unanswered, but the legacy is beyond dispute. Like Jimi Hendrix and many of the great blues guitarists who inspired him, Roy Buchanan was a singular artist who exposed his innermost self to the public through his music and ended up paying the ultimate price in return.

The Blues Guitar Style of Roy Buchanan

Roy Buchanan could squeeze more sounds out of a guitar with just his pinky finger on the volume knob and the edge of his pick than virtually anyone else. Not only that, but he could blaze up and down the fretboard with such velocity that the notes blurred into a "wall of sound," not unlike the "sheets of sound" ascribed to tenor sax giant John Coltrane. However, when playing the "*bluz*" he was fully capable of staying within the technical bounds of mere mortals while still expressing himself with startling intensity. Along with Albert Collins, James Burton, and a few others, Roy was most closely associated with the plebian Fender Telecaster. The justly prized 1953 model was his "best voice," though he toyed with Les Pauls (P-90 and humbucking varieties), a Strat, and near the end of his life, custom-made Teles.

Track 5 is a slow blues in the "country blues" key of E. Check out his work in the open 6th-string root position in measures 1, 2, and 11. Drawing on inspiration that dates back to his initial fascination with the steel guitar, Roy could bend like nobody's business. It takes some serious hand strength to bend the A (4th) to B (5th) on string 3 at fret 2 in measure 1, regardless of string gauge. Likewise, superb string control is required to execute the ascending, multi-step bends in measure 3 and the descending line of bends in measure 9. Regarding note selection, Roy had a predilection for the blues-defining ♭7th note (D in the key of E, G in the key of A, and A in the key of B) as shown in measures 2 (IV), 4 (I), 9 (V), 10 (IV), 11 (I and IV), and 12.

Performance Tip: Try pulling *down* on the G string with your index finger in measure 1. In measures 2, 3, and 10 use your ring finger *backed up* by the middle and index fingers. Bend the G at fret 15 and the E at fret 12 on beat 1 of measure 9 with your ring finger (don't forget the back up fingers), but use your index finger for the C♯ note at fret 9 and your middle finger for the A note at fret 10. Roy was the master of the "pinch harmonic" (P. H. in the notation), a subtle technique tricky to acquire. Hold the pick very tightly with just a fraction of the point showing beyond your fingertips. Strike the string with force and make sure that the tip of your thumb hits the string a split second behind the pick. Once you achieve the sound one time (perhaps by accident!) you will understand the process. Be aware that a fair amount of volume, distortion, and treble will help bring out these "zingers" or "whistlers," as they are sometimes called.

Roy would often play with considerable economy on uptempo blues such as the progression contained in Track 6. In measures 1–3 (I) he stays around the seventh fret, working the 9th (F#) up to the tart ♭3rd (G) with (mostly) languorous, half-step bends and only two brief resolutions to the root (E). Do not miss the extremely hip move in measure 1 where Roy adds in the ♭7th (D) on string 3 at fret 7 while simultaneously bending the 9th. Measure 4 (I) uses the "blues box" at fret 5 to access the root as well as the "sweet" 6th (C#) note. In measures 5 and 6 (IV chord, A) he also avoids the root (A), instead preferring to create musical tension by bending the 4th (D) to the 5th (E) and the 3rd (C#) to the 4th. Measure 7 (I) shows off an unusual bend of the #4th (A#) to the 5th (B) with release back to the #4th and a pull-off to the major 3rd (G#), thereby setting up the welcome resolution to the root on beats 2 and 4. Dig how Roy uses the A and G notes in measures 9 (V) and 10 (IV), with similar phrasing, to function as the ♭7th and #5th, and root and ♭7th notes, respectively.

Performance Tip: In measures 1–3 pull down on the F# notes with your index finger. This is virtually a necessity on beat 4 of the measure so as to not interfere with the D note on string 3.

Roy Buchanan Selected Discography

Roy Buchanan (Polydor)
Second Album (Polydor)
Live Stock (Polydor)
When a Guitar Plays the Blues (Alligator)
Sweet Dreams: The Anthology (Polygram)

"Blackie" talks back to "Slowhand" with a choice blue note.

ERIC CLAPTON
Crossroads

Though he was briefly called "Slowhand" in the Yardbirds due to his propensity for breaking strings followed by the slow, rhythmic clapping that would emanate from the impatient audience, Eric Clapton has never really needed a nickname. Just as Chet Atkins' being called "Mr. Guitar" was superfluous for a legend whose given name was enough to bespeak "country guitar," Clapton's is synonymous with blues-rock immortality. With the blues as his constant companion he has gone from mod London in the swinging sixties to sunny Miami in the laid back 1970s, from intense, private woodshedding on the electric guitar to the very public display of his acoustic chops on MTV. Compared to the other great guitarists of his generation, his many accomplishments, stature, and sheer longevity are nothing short of remarkable, with the legions of guitarists he has personally inspired second to none.

Eric Patrick Clapton was born on March 30, 1945 in his grandparent's Ripley home in Surrey, England. His sixteen-year old mother, Patricia Molly Clapton had an affair with Edward Walter Fryer, a twenty-four-year old Canadian soldier stationed in England, and Eric ended up being raised by his mother's parents, Jack and Rose Clapp (who had Patricia with her first husband, Reginald Cecil Clapton). Rose played piano, and Jack and an uncle were big band fans. Fryer, who sometimes played piano professionally, had returned to his wife back in Canada before his illegitimate son was born, and Patricia Clapton would go on to meet and marry another Canadian soldier, Frank McDonald, and follow him and his career to Canada and Germany. Young Eric grew up with the illusion that his grandparents were his parents, despite the difference in his and their last names. When he was nine his real mother, whom he had been brought up to think of as his older sister, returned to England for a visit with his half brother Brian. The shock of the revelation as to her true relationship to him would change the good, polite, and artistically inclined student into a withdrawn child with a loss of identity.

Clapton's grades suffered, and he was shuttled from school to school including the Holyfield Road School for art. In 1961 he entered the Kingston College of Art to pursue the study of stained glass making but was expelled after only two months for playing his guitar in class. His interest in the blues, R&B, and rock 'n' roll had become an all-consuming passion. In 1958 he had asked for a guitar for this thirteenth birthday upon hearing an album by Big Bill Broonzy and his discovery of the rock 'n' roll of Chuck Berry and Bo Diddley. Finding that it took too much effort to play the steel string acoustic with which he was presented, however, he put it down until he began college, and his grandparents helped finance a Kay copy of the Gibson ES-335. Ever the student of American roots music, he became obsessed with the acoustic country blues of Robert Johnson, Blind Boy Fuller, Son House, Skip James, Blind Lemon Jefferson, and then the electric stylings of Muddy Waters, Buddy Guy, and B.B., Albert, and Freddie King.

Flush with some proficiency, Clapton formed the Roosters with future Rolling Stones guitarist Brian Jones and future Manfred Mann members Tom McGuinness and Paul Jones. Within two months, however, the Roosters were history, and Clapton joined Casey Jones and the Engineers, a Mersey beat band from Liverpool. In a move that would be repeated over and over throughout his career, he left the "pop" group after two weeks as they offended his purist sensibilities. Meanwhile, the Rolling Stones, with ex-Rooster Brian Jones, had outgrown their local gig at the Crawdaddy Club in Richmond by 1963, leaving a void for the up-and-coming Yardbirds to fill. The Y-Birds had just axed their lead guitarist Anthony "Top" Topham and tapped Clapton for the post in October. By now he had a style based on a variety of sources including Chuck Berry and the West Side Chicago blues of Otis Rush, Magic Sam, and Buddy Guy. Short, stinging phrases—often beginning with a spiky bend—flowed from his Telecaster. Though not yet twenty years old, he already had a smooth, sensuous vibrato that would elicit praise from B.B. King (the inspiration) and Free's Paul Kossoff (the inspired, whom Clapton once asked in response to his slinky vibrato, "How do you do that?"). When the Yardbirds backed up Sonny Boy Williamson in 1963 he backpedaled to T-Bone Walker for a role model, though Sonny Boy would probably have wished to hear something more along the lines of his illustrious sidemen at Chess Records, the muscular and swinging Robert Junior Lockwood or the ripping Luther Tucker.

Though Clapton got to flash his hard-won blues licks on Chicago-style numbers like Billy Boy Arnold's "I Ain't Got You" and the original instrumental "Got to Hurry," Yardbirds lead singer Keith Relf had his eye on the prize. Clapton was gone after eighteen months in March 1965, just as the band was hitting the charts with "For Your Love." With his reputation growing among London's underground blues community, however, a month later in April he was asked to join John Mayall's Bluesbreakers, and history was to be made. Concurrent with the gig was a paradigm-shifting change of instruments. Where the trebly Tele had served him well in evoking the bright and reverbed West Side sound, he now played a sunburst 1960 Les Paul Standard with PAF humbucking pickups. In perhaps a happy accident, Clapton thought he was emulating Freddie King, who in the 1950s had actually wielded a '53–'55 Les Paul Gold top with single coil P-90 pickups. When Clapton mated the 'burst to a 1965 Marshall JTM 45 combo amp with two 12" speakers, the fatter, warmer, higher output 'buckers helped create a sound that rocked the guitar world. The result was almost magical—a thick, singing lead sound that thrilled fans and fellow guitarists alike. Along with Mike Bloomfield back in the States, who was making a similar discovery with his "Lester," Clapton set in motion a demand for "old" Les Paul guitars that would eventually mutate into the vintage guitar market. In addition, though traditional blues guitarists were not as turned on to try the LP/Marshall combination, rock guitarists dug the raw vibe, and a whole musical trend would spring out of it in the 1970s.

The power and glory unleashed on *John Mayall and the Bluesbreakers featuring Eric Clapton* in 1965 established him as a bona fide guitar hero of major proportions and convinced many a young, aspiring blues guitarist to approach the instrument with more aggression. His take on "All Your Love (I Miss Loving)" by Otis Rush displayed the same serpentine lines that would ignite envy in countless budding string benders, while "Ramblin' on My Mind" gave the guitarist a chance to play and sing the Robert Johnson classic his own way. Such was the feverish pitch of adulation for him that fans began scrawling the "Clapton is God" graffiti on walls and buildings in old London town that would come to haunt him. Though he always bemoaned that kind of idolatry, he did nothing to discourage it with his next project. In June of 1966 a casual event occurred that would shift the rock world on its axis. Drummer Ginger Baker sat in with Mayall's band, joining the recently hired bassist Jack Bruce in the rhythm section. Clapton had a musical epiphany and asked Bruce and Baker to follow his "lead" in forming the heavy blues-rock power trio Cream, containing the "world's greatest guitarist, bassist, and drummer." With their voluminous Marshall stacks, lengthy (some would say self-indulgent) onstage jams, and cocksure attitude, they gave everyone on both sides of the Atlantic Ocean the opportunity to hear one of the guitar's most enduring "voices" when *Fresh Cream* was released in December. Retiring the Les Paul Standard (though he man-handled a black Custom in the studio), Clapton now flaunted a cherry red, early sixties ES-335, a psychedelic, rainbow-painted Gibson SG, a Les Paul Special (with P-90s), and even a Gibson Firebird.

Besides giving him room to stretch his improvisations beyond the natural boundaries governed by the traditional 12-bar blues format *and* John Mayall's orthodoxy, being in Cream compelled him to develop his rhythm chops. Of course, a critical jab from Jimi Hendrix that he "did not play rhythm guitar" also helped to convince him to expand his vocabulary beyond basic open and barre chords. Despite the delirious reception of the fans (and record company execs who loved the infusion of cash that they brought), Cream was together for only three years and three classic albums of burning blues-rock riffing, though it was way longer than any other Clapton band before or since. The group collapsed under the weight of its own hype and the competing egos engendered by three full-time "soloists" and gave up the ghost of the late, lamented Cream in 1969. Jumping from the proverbial frying pan into the fire, however, Clapton allowed himself to be seduced into forming another "supergroup," Blind Faith (how ironic a name!), with Steve Winwood, Ginger Baker, and bassist Rick Grech from Family. Their one self-titled LP in 1970 had some tantalizing moments and signaled Clapton's continuing desire to expand his horizons beyond the blues, as the folk rock of "Can't Find My Way Home," a nylon-string guitar duet with Winwood, can now be seen as the seed for the MTV *Unplugged* session some twenty years off. Before the year was out "blind faith" was not enough to keep the super egos from clashing. They broke up after a pressure-filled, sold out American tour, and Clapton went off and recorded his first solo album. Bereft of blues and guitar heroics (to the utter dismay of many fans), it nonetheless showed his developing vocal chops and songwriting ability with "Let It Rain," a composition that would foreshadow the epic "Layla" two years hence. Produced by Southern rocker Delaney Bramlett, it also contained the American musicians who would become the Dominos behind "Derek." As an interim step, though, Clapton went on the road and recorded with Delaney and his wife Bonnie in a loose aggregation known as Delaney & Bonnie and Friends. Not insignificantly, Clapton made a seismic guitar switch to the Strat as reflected in his thinner, brighter sound.

In that busy and seminal year of 1970, the now "solo" Clapton put together Derek & the Dominos. Their one studio album, the monumental *Layla and Other Assorted Love Songs* was a thinly-disguised (thanks to the gossip in the rock press) bittersweet valentine that sprung from his unrequited (at the time) love for Patti Harrison, the wife of his good buddy George. It also provided the opportunity for Clapton to meet and become friends with Duane Allman, who shared drugs and swapped epic solos (and contributed the signature rhythm riff to "Layla") on the unparalleled artistic highpoint of Clapton's career. Again he failed to hold a band together, and after a live album but an unsuccessful attempt to record a followup studio album, the Dominos fell apart. Crushed by the commercial failure (at the time) of Layla and nursing a broken heart while he carried a flame for Patti Boyd Harrison (whom he would eventually marry in 1979 and divorce in 1988), Clapton descended into isolation and the living hell of heroin addiction for the next three years. Going so far as to even sell his guitars to finance his habit, he still managed to record demo tapes on his country estate and was lured back into performing again in 1973 at the Rainbow Theater in London by Pete Townshend. A year later he went to Miami, Florida and tracked the #1 charting *461 Ocean Boulevard* with the #1 single, reggae legend Bob Marley's "I Shot the Sheriff," debuting his new, clean, streamlined Southern sound and his new addiction, alcohol. Struggling with the disease that negatively affected his music as well as his life for almost a decade, he was hospitalized for ulcers due to the excessive consumption of brandy and painkillers, finally getting straight after controversial electro-acupuncture treatment suggested by Townshend in 1982. He toured and recorded with regularity, and while no longer the stone bluesman of yore, the live *E.C. Was Here* from 1975 was a thrilling slice of the old Slowhand. It literally burst with long, spectacular blues solos fueled by thick, Gibson humbucker distortion, though he would quickly return to his new main squeeze, the ubiquitous Fender Stratocaster. In 1985 he was a big hit at *Live Aid*, adding to his loyal fan base with a new, younger, pop-rock oriented audience.

In what would come too close to blues clichés about suffering, tragedy entered Clapton's life in a big way in the nineties. In August of 1992 Stevie Ray Vaughan and members of Clapton's road crew died in a helicopter crash following a gig in the midst of an all-star tour that also featured Buddy Guy and Robert Cray. In March of 1991 his five-year old son Conor died after falling out of a window in his mother's apartment in Manhattan. Fortunately, rather than turning to substance abuse for solace, he turned his grief into "Tears in Heaven" (Grammy) that appeared on *Unplugged* (#1 album, Grammy) along with covers of "Layla" and the blues in 1992. More importantly for his mental health and his legacy, in 1994 he finally recorded the all-blues album for which fans had been waiting an eternity. *From the Cradle* (#1 album), though conservative by the standards that virtuoso Stevie Ray Vaughan and his followers had established, was a loving tribute to his blues heroes, containing classics by Freddie King, Muddy Waters, Elmore James, Charles Brown, Lowell Fulson, and others.

1998's *Pilgrim* (Grammy for Best Pop Album) was his first album of new material in nine years, and like *Reptile* (an affectionate term for his uncle) from 2001, it showed the pop side of his personality that has warred uneasily with his bluesman's soul since the Yardbirds. In between, however, he realized another long-held goal when he recorded *Riding with the King* (#1 album) with B.B. King in 2000. A stunning commercial success with generally positive reviews, it once again proved the rap on Clapton that he often needed a little competition to bring out his best, whether that be Steve Winwood, Duane Allman, Albert Lee, or the "King" himself.

In a class by himself, Eric Clapton, the reluctant blues guitar hero and suave, Armani-suited pop star, is still a force to be reckoned with after forty years. As the only triple-inductee (at this point in time) into the Rock and Roll Hall of Fame for the Yardbirds, Cream, and his solo career, his immortality is assured in the public arena and in the hearts of guitar lovers everywhere.

The Blues Guitar Style of Eric Clapton

Rolling Stone magazine once conducted a blindfold test with Les Paul in the 1970s involving contemporary electric guitar players where Les was to put the albums he liked the best in a separate stack. At the end of the exercise Eric Clapton was represented far above his contemporaries, to which Les replied that, "…he tells a little story with every lick." Combined with his silky smooth vibrato, tone, and commanding chops, Eric Clapton has established one of the most recognizable styles in blues and rock. Though he has gone through Fender Teles, Gibson Les Pauls, Firebirds, ES-335s, and Explorers, the Strat has been his fave for over thirty years and he, too, now has a signature model.

Track 7 is a slow blues full of Eric's passionate phrasing and dramatic use of musical space. In measures 1–4 (I = A) and 5 (IV = D), he manipulates the blues scale in the "extension" position at fret 8, affectionately known as the "Albert King box," to his fine advantage. As usual for the blues, the note of resolution over the I is the root (A). The tension-producing tones, however, include the root bent to the ♭3rd (C), major 3rd (C♯), and ♭9th (A♯), in addition to the ear-twitching, half-step double-string bend (a Clapton trademark) of C/G (♭3rd and ♭7th) in measure 4. Notice the two-part bend of the root (D) to the ♭9th (D♯) and 9th (E), along with the quarter-step bend of the ♭7th (C) in measure 5 (IV). After shifting down to the 6th-string root position of the A blues scale in measure 6 (IV), Eric continues resolving to the root note (emphasized with glassy vibrato) while executing classic bends of the ♭3rd (C) to the major 3rd (C♯) and to the "true blue" note, in-between the ♭3rd and major 3rd in measure 7. Do not miss the subtle, chromatic move in measure 8 (I) of ♭7th–major 7th–root (G–G♯–A). In measures 10 (IV) and 11 and 12 (turnaround) Eric jumps the octave to the basic box of the blues scale at the seventeenth fret. In this register the bend from the ♭7th (C) to the root (D) in measure 10 is stunning, as is the corresponding bend of the ♭7th (G) to the root (A) on beat 4 of measure 10 in anticipation of the I chord in measure 11.

Performance Tip: The great "Slowhand" is a confirmed three-fingered player, thereby using his ring finger for virtually all bends. In measure 4, though, make the double-string bend more efficient by pushing up both strings with your index finger.

TRACK 7

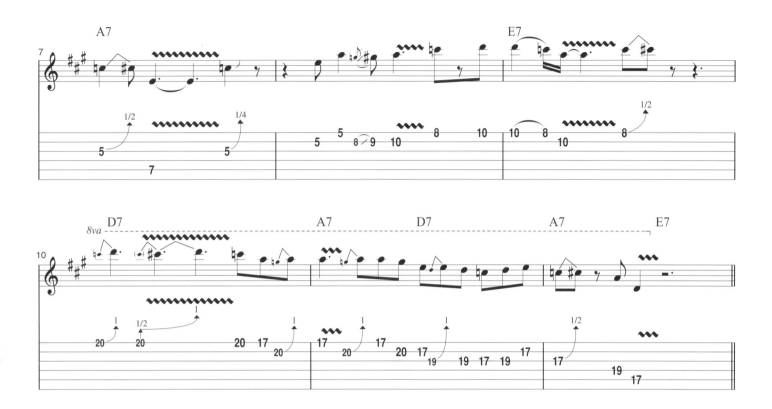

Eric takes a different scale approach in the moderate shuffle of Track 8 by working his way up the fingerboard to two of the less-used positions at fret 10 and fret 13. Over the I chord (G) in measures 1–3, he romps in the 6th-string root position of the blues scale with special attention to root (G) and ♭3rd (B♭—bent a quarter or a half step). Dig the unusual bending of the ♭3rd on string 5, at fret 1 in measure 3. In measure 4 (I) he begins a relocation to the "B.B. King box" (with roots on the 5th string, 10th fret and 2nd string, 8th fret) with the 9th (A) included from the composite blues scale (blues scale plus Mixolydian mode) that continues into measure 5 over the IV chord (C). In measure 6 (IV), however, he steps out of character to play a phrase all on string 2 that leads off with the ♭7th (B♭) bent to the root (C) on beat 1. Measure 7 (I) shows Eric bending the 9th a half step to the ♭10th (B♭) followed by a pull-off that resolves logically to the root (G). Following in measure 8 (I) he moves up the fingerboard to the tenth position blues box where he employs the 4th (C) and ♭3rd (B♭) notes for tension. Observe how this form allows easy access to the ♭7th (C) bent to the root (D) as well as the ear-bashing ♭6th (B♭) on beat 2 of measure 9 (V chord, D). In measure 10 (IV), Eric sashays to eleventh position for the blues box. He engenders hip tension by bending the root of the IV chord (C) to the 9th (D) and then descends to skillfully resolve to the root (G) on beat 1 of measure 11 (I). On beats 3 and 4 (IV) of measure 11, Eric highlights the root (C) before dramatically and dynamically dropping back to the G scale at fret 3 in measure 12 to eventually nail the G and D (4th and root) notes on beat 4. Check out the extremely unusual (but highly dynamic) move from the ♭3rd (B♭) bent to the "blue note" at fret 11 followed by the bend of the 4th (C) to the 5th (D) at fret 5!

Performance Tip: Bend the root (C) at fret 13 on beat 1 of measure 10 with your ring finger (backed up by the middle and index fingers) while accessing the 4th (F) with your pinky finger. This will put your hand in an advantageous position to access the ♭7th (B♭) note at fret 11 on beat 3. This is probably not how E.C. did it, but it is much more efficient than his "primitive" (!) fingering method.

TRACK 8   **Moderate Shuffle** ♩ = 120

Eric Clapton Selected Discography

With John Mayall and the Bluesbreakers:

John Mayall and the Bluesbreakers featuring Eric Clapton (Mobile)

With Cream:

Wheels of Fire (Atco)

With Derek & the Dominoes:

Layla and Other Assorted Love Songs (Polydor)

Solo:

E.C. Was Here (Polydor)

From the Cradle (Reprise)

RORY GALLAGHER
Emerald Isle Blues

It stands to reason that with the Irish people being a passionate, literate lot with a history of suffering at the hands of the British, they would produce a blues guitarist of great merit. Though there are more than one, Rory Gallagher would head any list. With a dedication to his old, battered Strat that was only exceeded by his love of the music itself, he left behind a body of work that reflects his personal insights and expression for the art form that he understood well.

Rory Gallagher was born on March 2, 1949 in Ballyshannon, County Donegal, Ireland, but moved to Cork City with his family not long after. He grew up hearing traditional Irish music and apparently went around the house singing as a little kid. On the radio he also heard the American pop songs of the day as performed by people like Guy Mitchell, Jo Stafford, and Tennessee Ernie Ford. In the mid-1950s

Photo by Richard Aaron

It is likely that Rory Gallagher is not playing "Danny Boy" on his beloved, pre-CBS Strat.

he became aware of the rock 'n' roll of Bill Haley and Elvis, though he was still too young to act on the change that was coming to him through the radio. Around 1958 he discovered the blues and folk music that was also edging its way onto the airwaves. Even more significant was his growing interest in skiffle music as performed by the reigning hero of the British Isles, Lonnie Donegan. From Donegan he was able to draw a line to Leadbelly and Woody Guthrie and was inspired to buy a cheap acoustic guitar. He bought a few of the available chord books and immediately went about the task at hand of learning how to play and sing. Gallagher formed a skiffle band with his brother Donal and spent 1959 performing on the Sunday Night Boy Scout variety show circuit and entering talent contests.

Two years later he bought his first electric, a funky Rosetti Solid VII along with a tiny Selmer Little Giant amp. Gradually his tastes began drifting to the early rock 'n' roll of first and foremost Buddy Holly, Chuck Berry, Jerry Lee Lewis, Eddie Cochran, and Fats Domino. An experience at his Christian Brothers school where he was severely chastised for having the audacity to play "Livin' Doll" by Cliff Richards would have a profound effect on the sensitive individual, causing him to realize that life might be a struggle for a musician with his convictions. His mother was aware of his talent and determination and allowed him to change to a school where he would not be penalized for his interests and for the occasional tardiness due to playing at night. Frustrated with trying to start his own successful group, at fifteen he joined the Fontana Showband that provided him with the regular opportunity to play in front of an audience and travel around the Irish countryside to a degree. It was also at this time that he acquired a Strat like his hero Buddy Holly had played. A '59 or '60 model sunburst, Gallagher believed it was the second Strat to be imported to Ireland, and he played it non-stop for years, as evidenced by the extreme wear—and resulting character.

The Showband was not his ideal situation, but at least he was able to play approximately 50 percent rock 'n' roll along with a selection of comedy material, pop dance numbers, and country and western. They eventually began performing around Belfast where a beat music scene was springing up. Gallagher commandeered control of the Fontana band, renaming it the Impact Showband and turning it into an R&B combo even while becoming aware of the Beatles and particularly the Rolling Stones.

Jeff Beck, Davey Graham, Bert Jansch, and Steve Winwood (on guitar) were also starting to gain a reputation locally, and Gallagher was compelled to explore the roots of the raunchier music they were playing. Like many others after him on both sides of the Atlantic, this curiosity led back to Muddy Waters, John Lee Hooker, Jimmy Reed, and all the great electric blues guitarists who followed in B.B. King's footsteps. Despite his band's flashier name, however, Gallagher was tiring of the routine and left the group in 1965. Within a matter of weeks the whole band split up, leaving bassist Eric Kitringham and drummer Norman Damery free to indulge their love of blues with Gallagher, and they went to Germany as a nameless blues power trio before calling themselves Taste.

Between 1966 and 1968 the trio gigged relentlessly with numerous forays into London, where they struggled to find gigs, in Ireland and across the English Channel to Hamburg, Germany, where the pastures were greener. In 1968 they relocated to London, working at the Marquee Club (where they recorded a live album that was not released until 1977) and festivals. By this time Kitringham and Damery had been replaced by Charlie McCracken from the Spencer Davis Group and John Wilson from Van Morrison's Them. They released two collector's albums called *Taste* (1969), with extended jams, and *On the Boards* (1970) that featured a wider variety of music than Cream was performing at the time (though they were clearly patterned after Clapton, Bruce, and Baker's virtuosic ensemble) with Gallagher contributing "tasty" harp and alto saxophone (!) to a couple of tracks. They opened for Blind Faith on the supergroup's star-crossed American tour in 1970 and also had the dubious honor of playing at the doomed Isle of Wight Festival the same year. By early 1971, however, Taste had disbanded, leaving *Live Taste* and *Live at the Isle of Wight* behind with the two studio albums.

Gallagher immediately threw himself into jump-starting a solo career by recording *Rory Gallagher* at the end of 1970. From 1971 on he would go out on tour and record under his own name with bassist Gerry McAvoy playing with him for years and years. *Deuce* (1972), *Live in Europe* (1972), *Blueprint* (1973), *Tattoo* (1973), *Irish Tour* (1974), *Calling Card* (1976), *Photo Finish* (1978), and *Jinx* (1982) came out in rapid succession until he took a breather from the continual globe trotting. In 1987 he picked up the pace again with *Defender* followed by his last album, *Fresh Evidence* in 1991. The albums were uneven, and the critics basically ignored him as time went on, though his obsessive commitment to getting it right, often in direct confrontation with management, record companies, and band members, produced some great blues guitar music. Perhaps tellingly, some of his most admired work was in the employ of others, like when he appeared on Muddy Waters' *London Sessions* (1972) and with Albert King on *Live* (1977) when "taste" rather than technique dictated the musical outcome.

In 1991 Gerry McAvoy and drummer Brendan O'Neill left Gallagher to form Nine Below Zero. With the unwavering tenacity that drove him to play music at the expense of everything else, including a normal social and family life, he picked himself right back up with a new rhythm section. In late 1994, however, after years of heavy alcohol abuse, he became seriously ill and died on June 14, 1995 following complications from a liver transplant. Though his name rarely comes up when exemplary plectrists are discussed, Rory Gallagher sold over 14 million records and often topped critic's polls over Eric Clapton. On the live recordings particularly, he left a legacy of his deep love for the blues that does honor to the legends that inspired him.

The Blues Guitar Style of Rory Gallagher

While Rory Gallagher did not develop a particularly distinctive style or tone, he had the energy and instinctive feel to produce solos of great power (and subtlety, when required) and a melodic sense shared with other British blues practitioners. His love affair with his battered pre-CBS Strat is well documented visually and aurally.

Track 9 finds the Irish guitar hero on the road less traveled in the key of C. Rory uses the C blues scale and the relative minor A blues scale with a kind of rough poetry that would do his fellow countryman (and fêted literary lion) Dylan Thomas proud. In measures 1–3 over the I chord (C) he starts out establishing the tonality by unambiguously nailing the root (C). In measure 3 he gets a jump on the IV chord (F) in measures 5 and 6 by playing the F and E♭ notes. Rory drops down to C major pentatonic at fret 5 in measure 4 and combines the root (C) and 6th (A) for a sweet, consonant sound. Staying in the same position for the IV chord in measure 5, he converts the A to the major 3rd and the C to the 5th of F, maintaining the harmonious effect begun in the previous measure. The following measure of the IV chord finds him back in the C blues scale where he spins triplets involving the ♭9th (F♯), ♭7th (E♭), and 5th (C) notes. In measures 7 and 8 (I) Rory plays similar licks before running down the scale to end up dynamically resolving an octave lower on the root. He pulls a fast one in measure 9 over the V chord (G), however, when he shifts decisively to the G composite blues scale (blues scale plus Mixolydian mode) for a change of keys. The IV chord is satisfactorily acknowledged in measure 10 in the extension position ("Albert King box") of the G blues scale with the 6th (D), 4th (B♭), 9th (G), and root (F). Rory resolves to the root (C) with a classic triplet lick, then rips off sixteenth-note licks containing the B♭, G, and F notes that function as the ♭7th, 5th, and 4th of C, and the 4th, 9th, and root of F in measures 11 and 12 of the turnaround, ratcheting up the tension for a big finish. After a tart bend of the ♭3rd (B♭) to the 4th (C) over the V chord on beat 3 for one last shot of musical tension, Rory resolves down to the root (G) on beat 4.

Performance Tip: Virtually all the bends could be executed with the ring finger. For the sixteenth-note licks in measures 11 and 12 use your pinky for the B♭, your index for the G, and your ring finger for the F notes.

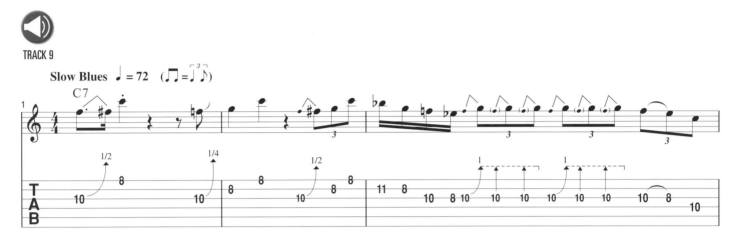

TRACK 9

Slow Blues ♩ = 72

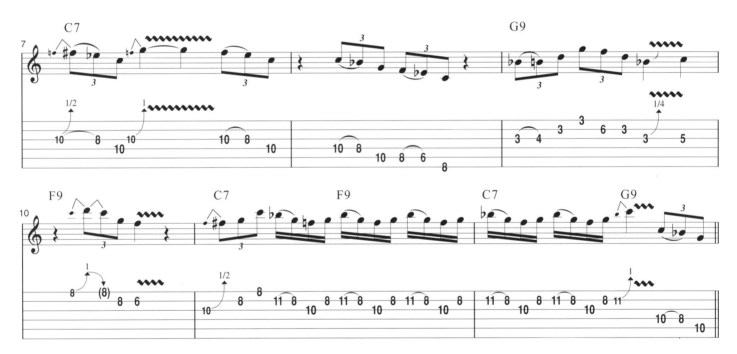

Rory boogies with economy in Track 10 while contrasting long, sustained notes with short bursts. That half-step bend in the extension position of the A blues scale to the sweet and tonality-defining major 3rd (C♯) in measures 1 and 2 over the I chord (A) sets the "tone" for the solo. Dig how he keeps repeating the major 3rd with additional bends in measures 3 and 4 and even into measure 5 over the IV chord (D), where C♯ functions as the major 7th, a perhaps unintentional nod towards Rory's jazz roots. The octave jump of the major 3rd (F♯) in measure 6 (IV) in the "B.B. King box" is a dynamic surprise that leads smoothly into measure 7 (I) and the composite blues scale (blues scale plus Mixolydian mode). The repetition of the ♭7th (G) in measure 8 (I) is a great set up for the V (E) that follows in measure 9. Long, looping, and sustained bends of the 4th (A) to the 5th (B) in measure 9 are held over into the IV chord (D) in measure 10, where the B functions as the sweet 6th. Rory keeps the tension up with the 4th (D) in measure 11 before closing out his blues chorus as it began—with the major 3 (C♯) in measure 12. Dig that there is no turnaround, just the harmony of the I chord to maintain the forward momentum and drive of the progression.

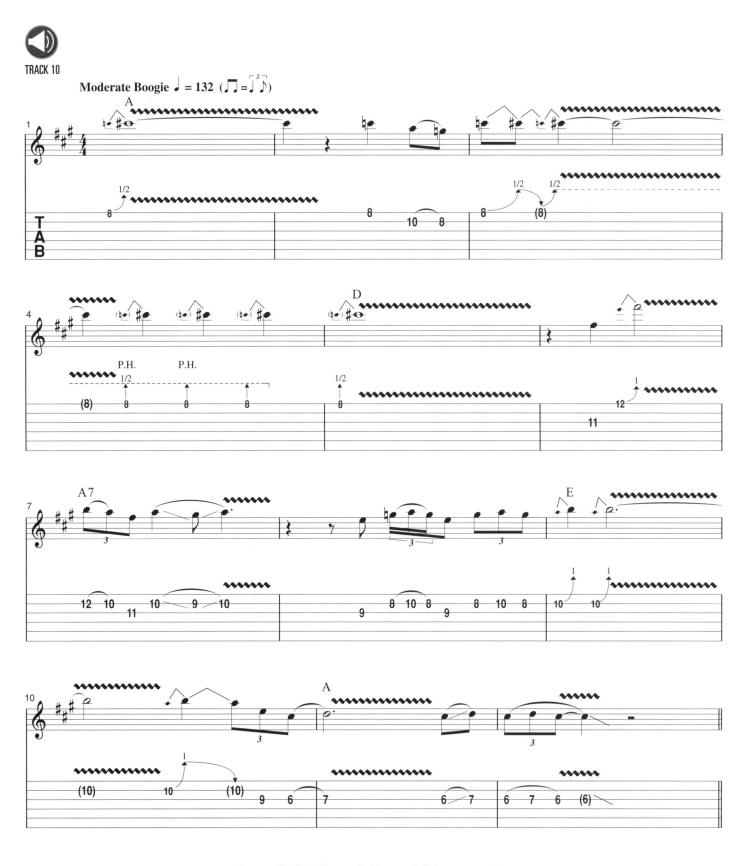

Rory Gallagher Selected Discography

With Taste:

On the Boards (Atco)

Solo:

Live in Europe (Buddha)

Irish Tour (Buddha)

Dreaming of "Tush?" A beardless Billy Gibbons fondling "Pearly Gates,"
his vintage Gibson Les Paul 'Burst.

BILLY GIBBONS
Sharp Dressed Man

"Ah how, how, how, how!" In 1973 you could not turn on the radio (FM *or* AM) or walk into a jam session without hearing Billy "F." Gibbons or a reasonable facsimile thereof growling that exhortation. ZZ Top had crossed over to the commercial rock world with "La Grange," arguably the best and most authentic tribute to John Lee Hooker and his famous boogie beat. Of course, not everyone realized the lineage; in fact, a reviewer for *Rolling Stone* thought Gibbons was imitating Leadbelly (!). No matter, however, the point was the music, and it struck a big fat "A" chord with fans and players alike at a time when the "sensitive, singer-songwriter" movement was just picking up steam. In short, it was a welcome blast of pure, unadulterated Texas blues-rock from an ass-kicking power trio, served up piping hot and spicy like a jalapeño burrito from south of the border.

Head honcho and git-picker deluxe, William Gibbons was born September 16, 1949 in Houston, Texas into a wealthy family. A Christmas present of a Gibson Melody Maker and a Fender Champ amp set him on the path to the blues via Jimmy Reed, Bobby "Blue" Bland, and Little Richard after allegedly being exposed to R&B music by the household's African-American maid. Around the age of fourteen in 1963 he began playing in a string of blues bands including the Saints, the Coachmen, and Billy & the Ten Blue Flames. In 1966 the singer/guitarist formed a psychedelic/blues combo with Tom Moore (keyboards), Don Summers (bass), and Dan Mitchell (drums) dubbed the Moving Sidewalks, and the garage rockers released Gibbons's "99th Floor" b/w "What Are You Going to Do" in 1967 on Tantara Records. It became a regional hit, and another 45 RPM platter was issued later in the year on Wand Records. More significantly, Gibbons met future manager Bill Ham, a local promoter, backstage at a Doors concert in Houston. The Sidewalks were soon booked to open for Jim Morrison & Co. on their Texas tour, which led them to a big time score opening for the Jimi Hendrix Experience in June 1968. The Voodoo Child was mightily impressed, giving young Billy boy a late 1950s pink Stratocaster as a gift and making mention of him being his favorite guitarist when queried by Johnny Carson on the *Tonight Show* later on. In 1969 the Sidewalks' lone LP *Flash* came out, but Moore and Summers were drafted and sent to Vietnam, and Lanier Grieg was brought in on keys for the swan song of the band.

Gibbons and Bill Ham set out to find the right backing musicians for a new group now named ZZ Top. According to Gibbons the name was either derived from a combination of Zig Zag and Top rolling papers, bluesman Z.Z. Hill, or an old, deteriorating billboard with the two words mashed together. The longhaired fans of the band have always opted for the first possibility. Whatever the reality, after forays down several blind alleys, Gibbons met two Dallas cats, bassist Dusty Hill (born May 19, 1949) and drummer Frank "Rube" Beard (born June 11, 1949). Hill, with guitarist brother Rocky, had been in the Warlocks with Beard since the early sixties, changing their name to American Blues in 1967, at one point dyeing their hair blue for good measure. They had released a number of singles and LPs, but could not break out beyond the confines of the Lone Star State and had recently disbanded. Beard joined Gibbons first in a very early incarnation of the band, but found that he was not happy working with another bassist, and Hill was brought in to complete the triumvirate in February of 1969. Several years of knocking around the big "T" playing penny-ante gigs, including at the Beaumont Knights of Columbus Hall, would transpire until the seventies.

Ham secured financing from Houston record producer Pappy Daily, and *ZZ Top's First Album* saw daylight on the London label. Though Ham's liner notes blathered on pretentiously about "abstract blues," the disk was fairly straight-ahead electric Texas blues with a nod to Lightnin' Hopkins and glancing acknowledgement of British blues circa John Mayall and the Bluesbreakers with Eric Clapton. *Rio Grande Mud* from 1972, with hot riffs wedded to deep grooves and a sly wit, provided a hint of the future, however, as stomping blues-rock like the hit "Francine," "Just Got Paid," and "Bar-B-Q" mixed with the southern funk of "Ko Ko Blue," "Chevrolet" (later covered by Straw Dog), "Whiskey 'N Mama," and "Down Brownie." "Apologies to Pearly" and "Sure Got Cold After the Rain Fell" showed the band's certifiable blues roots and featured Gibbons's jaw-dropping chops and killer tone. A year later, however, the ZZ Top bandwagon rolled into town whoopin' and hollerin' with their definitive outing. Pulled in by "La Grange," *Tres Hombres* added to the blues-rock lexicon with "Beer Drinkers & Hell Raisers" and "Waitin' for the Bus/Jesus Just Left Chicago." Soulful R&B like "Hot, Blue, and Righteous" and "Have You Heard" presented another side of Gibbons's prolific songwriting talents, while the cosmic "Master of Sparks," the funky "Sheik," and the progressive "Precious and Grace" stretched the bounds of the genre even farther. Often missed by reviewers and critics is Gibbons' witty, sardonic humor mixed in with the "party-hardy" attitude.

Tearing it up on the road convinced the guys to release a semi-live album in 1975 with *Fandango*. They were breaking one attendance record after another in the process of becoming one of the major arena rock acts of the seventies, and side one of the LP captured them getting down in New Orleans with extended workouts on "Thunderbird" and a "Backdoor Medley." Meanwhile, the flip side contained a selection of mostly short, radio-friendly tuneful numbers, including a tribute, "Heard It on the X," to the pirate radio station they heard in the mid-sixties. Also included were two future classics: the tongue-in-cheek slow minor blues, "Blue Jean Blues" (covered by Jeff Healey), and the outrageous, butt-rocking "Tush."

In conjunction with their exhausting year-and-a-half-long Worldwide Texas Tour that began in 1975 ("Zee Zee's" first bonafide road tour of any consequence), the mysterious, but aptly titled *Takin' Texas to the People* was released as a promo disk. The show was an unprecedented production with live-stock such as a buffalo and a longhorn steer, and the pesos rolled in. *Tejas* was put out in the interim and was regarded as a tepid step in their evolution, though tunes like "Arrested for Driving While Blind" and "El Diablo" had Gibbons reaching beyond the blues for an almost fusion sound. In what has become a part of the ZZ Top lore, the three hombres went their separate ways around the world for almost three years for a well-deserved break from the concert grind.

Degüello in 1979 signaled the Top's return to form with new vigor, a new label (Warner Brothers), and a host of classics like "Cheap Sunglasses," "I'm Bad, I'm Nationwide," and their saucy version of Sam & Dave's "I Thank You." Something else was afoot, or a "head," however, as the boys sported longish beards and shades on the album liner. With *El Loco* in 1981, the transition to something more ambitious than just a traditional Texas R&B persona was clearly in visual evidence as the beards got longer. Aurally, too, change was a'coming. Except for the surprisingly lovely ballad, "Leila," the tunes were fast and streamlined, such as the leering "Tube Snake Boogie" and the salacious "Pearl Necklace." The latter had more than raunch going for it, however. The condensed blues 'n' boogie was a harbinger of the band's upcoming commercial breakthrough of unparalleled proportions.

Of all the bands that one would expect to make it on MTV during the cable music channel's debut years in the early eighties, ZZ Top would have to be near the bottom of the list with southern boogie bands like Lynyrd Skynyrd, the Outlaws, and others of their ilk. *Au contraire*, amigos! With an eye (and ear) for marketing nothing short of brilliant, Gibbons & Co. parlayed even longer beards, boiler suits, funky-looking custom guitars, gorgeous women (girls), stripped-down, synthesizer-driven boogie grooves, and Billy's 1933 Ford coupe as a symbol and namesake of the multiplatinum smash *Eliminator* in 1983. "Gimme All Your Lovin'," "Sharp Dressed Man," and "Legs" kept the disk on the charts for 135 weeks. Two years later *Afterburner* dished up more of the same, and kids who had no idea of their "sordid" past as a blues band thought they were really cool. "Sleeping Bag," "Rough Boy," and "Velcro Fly" kept the hit singles on track.

Not counting the repackaging of their first six albums in *ZZ Top Six Pack* in 1987 (maintaining their two-year release schedule), it would take until 1990 for new material to arrive in the form of *Recycler*. Featuring "Doubleback," a theme song for *Back to the Future III* and the blues tribute of "My Head's in Mississippi," it eschewed the previous records' synth-orgy for an ear-popping array of "techy" electric guitar sounds and pertinently acknowledged the band's early blues crusade. It was noted that after twenty years in the saddle, the Top had sold over 50 million records. Being that the blues informed their best music, it was only right that some sort of payback was in order, and the three caballeros stepped right up. On a trip to the Delta Blues Museum in Clarksdale, Mississippi, they were taken to the tumbledown shack where Muddy Waters had been born. Snatching up a plank, Gibbons had it made into a guitar christened the "Muddywood," and it was sent on a nationwide tour of Hard Rock Cafes to raise money for the museum, where it now resides. Despite the clowning and goofs on the culture of the blues through the years, Gibbons, Hill, and Beard have always been serious students and interpreters of the form.

Like clockwork, in 1992 a *Greatest Hits* CD appeared with two previously unreleased singles, "Viva Las Vegas," and "Gun Love," but two years later Zee Zee made another major change. They switched labels to RCA in 1994 and brought out *Antenna*, a deliberate effort to lose the synthesizers and get back to their original riff-heavy, blues-rocking period epitomized by *Tres Hombres*. The same year, as if to underscore their commitment to their roots, a collection of their original blues compositions called *One Foot in the Blues* was also sprung on an unsuspecting public.

In 1996 *Rhythmeen* pushed the sands of time back even further as the raw thump of their classic sound was emphasized by the fact that the disk was the "first pure trio record of our career," according to Gibbons. Likewise, the title refers to "mean rhythm," and it is an accurate description of a disk that most folks feel was an improvement over *Antenna*. In January of 1997 the band played the halftime show at Super Bowl XXXI, and in October made an appearance on the *VH1 Fashion Awards*, playing—what else?—"Sharp Dressed Man."

ZZ Top's last release in 1999 commemorated their thirtieth anniversary with XXX. Featuring eight new studio tracks and four live cuts, it shows them standing proud and tall, unbowed after thirty years of tin-eared critics who originally compared them to Grand Funk and Kiss (!), the only band of their stature in that time to have survived without a single personnel change. A planned world tour in 2000 was cut short when Dusty Hill contracted hepatitis C, but his disease is now in remission, and the Top played at the Bush Inaugural in January of 2001. They toured Europe in late 2002 while planning a U.S. tour in 2003 along with the release of a new album.

The Blues Guitar Style of Billy Gibbons

Billy Gibbons is a fire-belching, tire-squealing blues and rock machine capable of eliminating the competition at the drop of a guitar pick. Instead of making gratuitous displays of fretboard power, however, he has consistently opted for the three T's: "taste, tone, and technique." He is, of course, best known for his vintage Les Paul sunburst "Pearly Gates," but also rides around in Strats, a Flying V, a Gretsch "Bo Diddley" square guitar, and custom made vehicles with fur, etc.

The slow blues of Track 11 shines a light on Billy's Lightnin' Hopkins influence. Dig that the entire solo takes place in the open position of the E minor pentatonic scale save for measures 1 and 2. Those two measures get the country blues vibe happening with the classic blues "train whistle" found in Robert Johnson's "Sweet Home Chicago," as well as being a signature lick of Po' Lightnin's primal style. Dig that this tension-skewing lick is resolved in measures 3 and 4 with the open E (root) string before being "taken up a notch" again in measures 5 and 6 over the IV chord (A) with the ♭7th (open D string), 5th (E), and 2nd (B) notes. Definite resolution occurs in measures 7 and 8 (I) where The Rev. Billy F. hammers to the tonality-defining major 3rd (G♯) combined with the root (E) in measure 7 and the root notes in measure 8. He then smartly walks up to the bass root (B) note in measure for the V chord (B) while picking a broken B7 voicing intensified with the repetition of the open B string. Check out the blues-approved 5th (F♯) of B on string 6 at fret 2. Measure 10 (IV chord, A) contains rich blues harmony with D/A (4th and root) and E/B (5th and 9th on strings 2 and 1 open) and the slick sequence of B–A–G (♭7th) on beats 3 and 4. A vibrant, improvised turnaround with an ascending and descending line is created in measures 11 and 12 with G♯/E and E/B identifying the I chord in measure 11 and the similar G♯ and E notes providing the same service on beats 1 and 2 of measure 12. The V chord is then implied by the classic walkup of ♭7th (A), 7th (A♯), and the root (B) on beat 3 of measure 12.

Performance Tip: Blow the train whistle in measures 1 and 2 with your middle finger bending string 2 and your index finger anchored on string 1.

Billy gets *down* to the boogie in Track 12 with lewd bends and tight clusters of aggressively picked notes in the hip key of B♭ (instead of the more proletariat A or E). In measures 1 and 3 Billy raises the ♭7th (A♭) to the root (B♭), the 4th (E♭) to the 5th (F) in measure 2, and the ♭3rd (D♭) to the 4th and the 5th in a screaming series of bends. In measure 9 over the V chord (F) and measure 10 over the IV chord he employs the spiky bend of the E♭ to F to function as the ♭7th and root and root and 9th, respectively. Billy keeps "the pedal to the metal" in measure 11 with the root (B♭) note beginning and ending the measure and then resolves to the root (F) of the V chord on beat 4 of measure 12.

Performance Tip: If you play the F and A♭ notes in measures 7 and 12 with your ring and middle fingers, respectively, it will put you in position for the following slide and pull-off figure. Execute the bend of D♭ to E♭ in measure 10 with your index finger.

Billy Gibbons Selected Discography

ZZ Top's First Album (Warner)

Rio Grande Mud (Warner)

Tres Hombres (Warner)

Fandango (Warner)

PETER GREEN
Green's Blues

To paraphrase B.B. King, "Peter Green is the only other guitar player who made me sweat." High praise indeed from the "King of the Blues," but one listen to early Fleetwood Mac in the late 1960s when they were the purest and toughest blues band in England will convince even the most jaded blues guitar fan. Besides the three "Ts"—taste, tone, and technique—"Greeny" had an especially deep soulfulness rarely approached even by his peers Eric Clapton, Mick Taylor, or Rory Gallagher. The tragic arc of his story only seems to add to the profound nature of his art.

Peter Alan Greenbaum was born on October 29, 1946 in London's East End to a poor, working class Jewish family. He started playing at ten when one of his brothers brought home a budget acoustic, showed him some chords, and passed on the cast off instrument to the enthusiastic youngster. B.B. King, Muddy Waters, Chuck Berry, Fats Domino, Bo Diddley, and Hank Marvin of Britain's beloved Shadows were seminal influences, along with "some old Jewish songs."

Photo by LFI

Peter Green about to conjure up his "Black Magic Woman" on a pre-CBS Strat.

By the age of fifteen Peter Greenbaum was calling himself Peter Green and playing bass. When he left school he became a butcher and played R&B with Bobby Denim and the Dominoes and pop music with the Muskrats. When Eric Clapton made his infamous sojourn to Greece in 1965 Green, with unbridled self-confidence, badgered John Mayall to allow him to take Slowhand's place. Giving in to the relentless requests for a chance to prove he was better than the replacement, Mayall allowed the brash teenager to sit in for approximately three gigs. By all accounts he acquitted himself with aplomb, but was aced out in November when Clapton returned from holiday. Green then played bass in the Tridents before joining Peter Bardens's band, known as Peter B's Looners, on lead guitar in 1965, where he made his recording debut with "If You Wanna Be Happy." The move was fortuitous as it introduced him to drummer Mick Fleetwood. The Peter Bees (as they were referred to by the cognoscenti) evolved into a large R&B revue with Rod Stewart on lead vocals, a situation that dismayed the blues purist Green. When Clapton left the Bluesbreakers to form Cream in 1966, Mayall remembered the talented Green and hired him to fill the young legend's shoes. Despite the often less than polite reception he received from Clapton's loyal fans, Green eventually won everyone over with his unique, heavily-vibratoed sound that relied as much on dynamic musical space as the actual notes played. Within a year Mick Fleetwood joined bassist John McVie in the rhythm section of the Bluesbreakers, setting the stage for the emergence of Fleetwood Mac in 1967. Meanwhile, Green's thrilling guitar rides, especially on the instrumental "Supernatural" that appeared on *A Hard Road*, moved him into the front ranks of British blues guitarists.

Green recorded an album with Chicago blues pianist Eddie Boyd before putting the initial version of FM together with second guitarist Jeremy Spencer (a dead-on bottleneck clone of Elmore James) and bassist Bob Brunning. A short while after the band's debut in August of 1967 bassist John McVie finally got out of his contract with Mayall's Bluesbreakers and put the "Mac" in Fleetwood Mac. In February of 1968 they released their eponymous debut album, *Peter Green's Fleetwood Mac* and immediately moved into the vanguard of the burgeoning British blues scene. Green, however, was already feeling his creative juices constrained by playing traditional blues with Elmore-obsessed Spencer and hired Danny Kirwan as yet a third guitarist to help expand the band's sound.

Mr. Wonderful (1968), *English Rose* (1969), *Then Play On* (1969), and the live *Boston Tea Party* (recorded in 1970, released in 1998) showed Green to be a brilliant songwriter as well as an extraordinary improviser. The dreamy, non-blues instrumental "Albatross" was a #1 hit single in England, while "Black Magic Woman" would go on to be the defining moment of Carlos Santana's career when he covered it in 1970. The band was a huge success, going to Chicago to record (much as the Stones had in the early 1960s) *Blues Jam at Chess* with Buddy Guy, Honeyboy Edwards, Willie Dixon, Big Walter Horton, and others (who, though skeptical of the young, skinny, white Englishmen at first, came to admire their authentic blues), but the effect on Green appeared to be detrimental. Combined with reckless experimentation with LSD, his behavior became bizarre and spiraled downward at a terrifying rate of speed. His autobiographical "Man of the World" and particularly the proto-heavy metal (later covered by Judas Priest) "Green Manalishi (with the Two Pronged Crown)," while striking instrumentally, attested to his depressed and deteriorating mental condition. He became disillusioned with the music business and all the trappings of fame and fortune. He appeared onstage in long robes with crucifixes around his neck. He declared that the band should give away its income above and beyond what was needed for subsistence, and he began to give away his possessions, including his guitars. In the summer of 1970 he left Fleetwood Mac, to the ultimate regret of his fellow musicians and devoted fans.

Green released a depressing, bitter solo album called *End of the Game* (1970) and rejoined the Mac briefly when Spencer suddenly split to become a member of the Children of God in Los Angeles. He guested on a number of albums, including the reformed and reconfigured FM, but jail time and confinement in an asylum where he received harsh, damaging treatment left him a shell of his former self. *In the Skies* (1979), *Little Dreamer* (1980), *White Sky* (1981), and *Colors* (1983) contained a few sparks of the old Greeny, but the spiral continued downward. People reported running into him on the streets of London in a ragged, disheveled state with his fingernails grown so long as to prevent playing. In 1997, with the generous help of concerned friends, he made another, more successful attempt to recover his past abilities with *Bandit* and the *Peter Green Splinter Group*. In 2003 he released *Destiny Road* and toured with the band. The album featured serviceable blues and blues-rock with Green taking more of a sideman role, a situation even more apparent in concert. A painful, yet somehow hopeful experience to behold, it reveals a man who looks lost among his band mates until every so often when the "switch" goes back on and for a brief, shining moment, a flash of the old Peter Green is glimpsed. One can only hope that with more time, encouragement, and proper treatment all around, he can fully return to a life that is fulfilling for him in all aspects.

The Blues Guitar Style of Peter Green

Peter Green clearly built his lead guitar style upon the pioneering work of B.B. King, but he added a personal dimension to it with his fluid, elastic phrasing that dripped of deep blues expression. On top of that he always flaunted a harmonically rich tone generated by his vintage Les Paul 'burst (now owned by Gary Moore) or pre-CBS Strat.

Track 13 spotlights the elegance and fire of his slow blues soloing. With a nod towards his "main man," Peter finesses the "B.B. King box" around fret 10 in measures 1–4 over the I chord (A). Though the root (A) functions as the point of resolution and appears with regularity as expected, Peter creates delicious musical tension with the 6th (F♯) in measure 2 and the 4th (D) and ♭3rd (C) in measure 4. He then remains in the "box" in measures 5 and 6 over the IV chord (D), where the F♯ and A notes now become the tonality-defining major 3rd and the 5th, respectively, in measure 5. In measure 6 the bend from the 6th (B) to the hip *major* 7th (C♯), the 9th (E) to the 10th (F♯), and the 6th to the ♭7th (C) fills four beats with melodic note choices. Peter moves down to the fifth position A blues scale in measures 7 and 8 (I) with emphasis on the major 3rd (C#) and root. For the V chord (E) in measure 9 he leaves plenty of musical space and surprises with a jazzy diad of a 3rd (E/C#) that functions as the root and 6th. Measure 10 (IV) is likewise sparse, with the 5th (A) and 6th (B) notes adding color to the dominant 9 chord change. For his turnaround in measures 11 and 12 Peter establishes the I chord with the root, nails the IV chord dominant tonality with cool 3rds of A/F# (5th and 3rd) and C/A (b7th and 5th). The 6th (F#), root (A), and 9th (B) notes command the I chord change in measure 12 with E/B cementing the V chord.

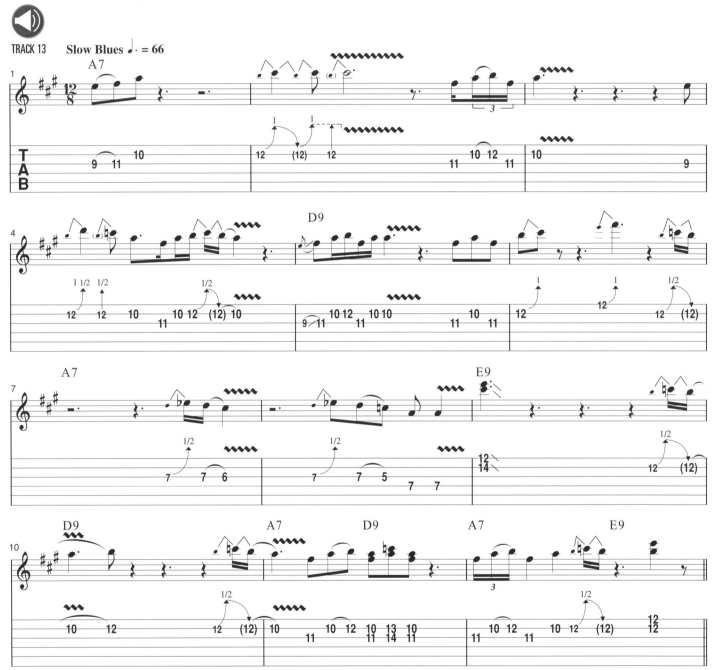

Perfectly content to spectacularly mine the territory that he knows best, Peter plays ten of the twelve measures of Track 14 in the "B.B. King box." The "fast change" to the IV chord (D) in measure 2 provides him with the opportunity to land squarely on the subdominant tonality with the 3rd (F#) and 5th (A) notes. Dig the inclusion of the b3rd (F) hammered to the major 3rd on beat 4, a classic blues move derived from the composite blues scale (blues scale plus Mixolydian mode). The hammer from the 6th (F#) to the b7th (G) in measure 3 (I) that is extended with vibrato is pure "blues deluxe." The I chord's dominant quality is echoed in measure 4 when Peter bends the 5th (E) to the b7th on beat 4.

Notice his use of the triadic tones of the root (D), 5th (A), and 3rd (F♯)—along with the jazzy 9th (E)—in measure 5 over the IV chord (D). Bending to the major 3rd (C♯), releasing to the 9th (B) and rebending to the major 3rd over the I chord in measure 7 creates an exquisite melodic line that resolves to the root via the spicy ♭3rd (C) note. In measure 9 over the V chord (E), Peter cops a lick right from B.B.'s overflowing bag of tricks with the bend of the root (E) to the 9th (F♯), bristling with tension, followed by a run down to the 4th (A) for extra bite. Ending on the 5th (A) in measure 10 (IV) adds a little musical tension while previewing the root (A) note on beat 1 of measure 11 in the 6th-string root pattern A blues scale at the fifth fret. The A/F♯ (5th and 3rd) dyad on beat 3 identifies the IV chord, while the fast, sixteenth-note triplet of ♭7th–6th-5th (C–B–A) on the same beat intensifies the dominant quality of the chord change. Classic blues double-stops in measure 12 with the always hip hammer-on from the ♭3rd (C) to the major 3rd (C♯) while sustaining the 5th (E) solidifies the I chord change as Peter resolves to the root (E) of the V chord on beat 4.

Performance Tip: Barre strings 3 and 2 at fret 5 in measure 12 with your index finger and hammer to the C♯ with your middle finger. Access F♯/D on beat 2 with your ring finger.

Peter Green Selected Discography

With John Mayall and the Bluesbreakers:

Hard Road (Mobile)

With Fleetwood Mac:

Peter Green's Fleetwood Mac (Blue Horizon)

English Rose (Epic/Sony)

Vintage Years (Sire)

Then Play On (Reprise)

Blues Jam in Chicago (Blue Horizon)

Live at the Boston Tea Party (Original)

BUGS HENDERSON
The Best Kept Secret in Texas

Maybe it is because of the sheer size of the area or the vast influx of immigrants from neighboring states, especially the musically fertile Mississippi, Alabama, and Arkansas. Whatever the reasons, Texas has produced an enormous number of great guitar players in accordance with its geographical prominence. Surprisingly, perhaps, some of the greatest slip through the commercial cracks of the music world. Bugs Henderson, more than anyone else, would have to be the prime candidate for, "You gotta hear this guy!" When he said in *Guitar Player Magazine*, "Give me a Fender Bassman and a Strat and I can blow anybody away," it was no idle boast. Had he managed his career better, he possibly could have garnered the fame of Stevie Ray Vaughan, Billy Gibbons, or Johnny Winter. Relatively young (he's fifty-nine as of this writing) for a blues cat, it could still happen, but it is not likely.

Buddy "Bugs" Henderson was born on October 22, 1944 in Palm Springs, California, but grew up in Tyler, Texas near Louisiana. He received a Montgomery Ward Airline guitar on Christmas Day, 1950 when he was six years old after exhibiting the telltale signs of a born player. By the late 1950s he was acquiring every guitar record he could find, with a special appreciation for James Burton when he played with teen idol Ricky Nelson. His tenure in a Tyler record store in the early 1960s gave him additional access to the hot vinyl he craved, including stacks of Ventures platters. Defying his father, Henderson would sneak out to the "joints" to hear live music, and at sixteen he formed his first garage band, the Sensors. Not long after, he joined his guitar-playing friend Ronnie Weiss in the folk-rocking Mouse and the Traps, and they relocated to Dallas. In 1966 they had a minor hit with "Public Execution," and during his stint in the band Henderson was dubbed "Bugs" due to his lightning speed on the fretboard—a "gift" that he has often tried to downplay to little avail!

By the late 1960s he was good enough to become the session guitarist at Robin Hood Studios (where ZZ Top would also record) on various rock and country dates. As the 1970s turned over Henderson found himsel ftotally immersed in and wild about the blues. In 1971, however, he returned to Tyler and joined a country band. Shortly thereafter he was contacted by Capitol Records guitarist and singer John Nitzinger who needed another picker to join him in the studio for *Thunder Thunder*. Touring with Texas rocker Nitzinger while opening for the Allman Brothers, Leon Russell, and B.B. King was an eye-opening experience, though he tired of the heavy riff-rock required of his abilities. Heeding the advice his friend and poker buddy Freddie King offered him, Henderson went out on his own in 1974 and formed a blues trio with Ron Thompson and Bobby Chitwood.

Photo by Carl Dunn

Looking more dapper than the typical Texas blues cat, Bugs Henderson casually rips the frets off his vintage Gibson ES-345.

Thirty years on with a succession of Shuffle Kings, Henderson has become a cult figure among guitarists who often make sojourns to catch his gigs in Texas, as he avoids extensive travel at all costs. Classic rock, fifties rock 'n' roll, instrumental rock, country music, swing jazz and, most importantly, blues both hot and sweet pour forth from his guitars in a torrent of notes that are always cleanly articulated and invested with feeling and killer tone. *The Bugs Henderson Group at Last* (1975) began the trek to mythological status with the all-blues jam *American Music* (1993), *Years in the Jungle* (1993), and the spectacular *Daredevils of the Red Guitar* (1994) displaying his fret-bending virtuosity along with his slyly drawling southern vocals and clever songwriting. American Music is Henderson's term of choice for his music, and the disk includes a string (pun intended) of guests with Johnny Winter, Willie Nelson, Jimmy Vaughan, and Ronnie "Mouse" Weiss lending their best licks. *Years in the Jungle* contains a passel of original blues and rock with "She Feels Good" sporting an astounding unaccompanied intro that slithers in and out of time like a diamondback rattler. *Daredevils of the Red Guitar* is an eclectic set with a brilliant Ventures medley, "Sweet and Mean," a classic slow blues with mind-warping solos and a blistering, head-snapping shuffle called, appropriately, "Jitterbugs."

The recordings of the last ten years have been a mixed bag to say the least, with inferior material, backing bands (including his son Buddy on drums) not up to his performance level, and a lack of direction contributing to his stasis in the music world. Most significantly, however, is his order of priorities that allowed him to recover from a period of "having too much fun" in the late 1970s: Family, music, and career. As he succinctly puts it: "I couldn't have the life I have now and be a major star. Couldn't go to my kids' ball games. I wouldn't give that up for anything." His family's gain and our loss. Seems fair.

The Blues Guitar Style of Bugs Henderson

Bugs Henderson can flat out blow through blues changes like a Texas tornado. Fast and clean, notes pour forth from his fingers in an overwhelming, but controlled, flood. At the same time, he is perfectly capable of easing back and making a few, choice blue notes speak volumes for him. Like all modern blues masters, he knows how to squeeze thick, warm tones out of any axe. He was seen with a Gibson ES-335 in the 1970s, but like most sons of the Lone Star State he generally slings a Strat along with an atypical Paul Reed Smith.

The slow blues of Track 15 has compressed energy pulsing from tightly packed note clusters and dynamic release resulting from longer, sustained scale degrees. Using the extension position, or "Albert King box," from the B♭ blues scale in measures 1 and 2 (I), Bugs bends the ♭3rd (E♭) through a variety of related pitches to create riveting tension while making regular forays to the root (B♭) for resolution. The 6th fret, 6th-string root position of the B♭ composite blues scale (blues scale plus Mixolydian mode) in measures 3 and 4 (I) finds ole' Bugs twisting sixteenth notes into long legato lines, including a tasty chromatic phrase on beat 2 of measure 3 that contributes to the impact of the measure. Oh, Mama! In measures 5 and 6 over the IV chord (E♭) he ladles in the root (E♭) note while ripping the hell out of the ♭7th (D♭) and the tonality-defining major 3rd (G). A welcome breather occurs in measure 7 of the I chord where Bugs extracts sweet sustain out of the major 3rd (D). Likewise, in measure 8 (I) he "simply" lets the 5th (F), 3rd (D), and ♭7th (A♭) notes imply the I7 tonality before heading off into a snakey series of repeating bends of the 2nd (G) to the melodic 3rd (A) in measure 9 over the V chord (F). Rippling sixteenth-note triplets in measure 10 (IV) include a slick blues scale arpeggio of the 5th (B♭), ♭7th (D♭), 9th (F), and octave 5th on beat 2. Bugs "rests" in the 6th-string root position of the B♭ blues scale for his turnaround in measures 11 and 12, economically emphasizing the I, IV, I, and V changes with the ♭7th (A♭), 5th (B♭), major 3rd (D), and 4th/root (B♭ and F) notes, respectively.

Performance Tip: There is no real tip for executing this type of virtuosity except to offer the advice to employ all four fingers of the left hand at all times!

TRACK 15

Slow Blues ♩ = 64 (♫ = ♩♪)

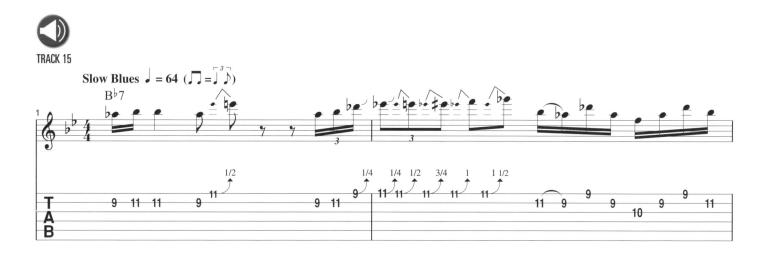

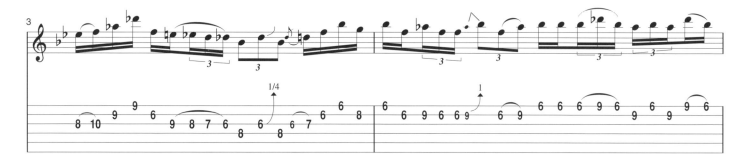

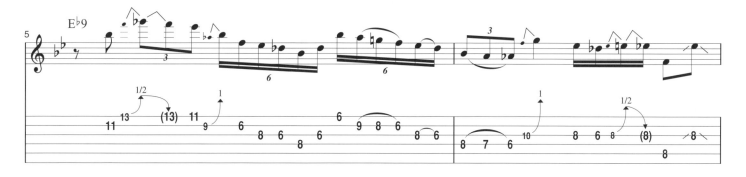

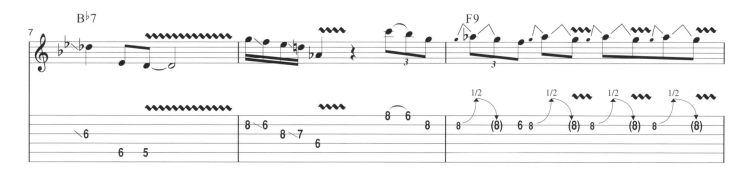

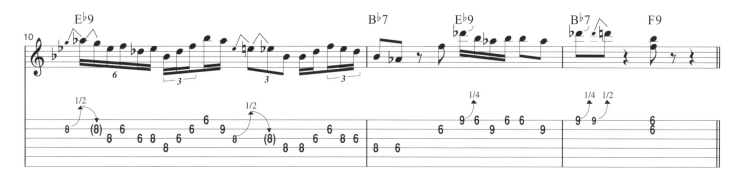

Conversely, after letting loose a torrent of notes over the slow blues, Bugs chooses to proffer a combination of quarter and eighth notes in the fast, swinging shuffle of Track 16. After entering by sustaining and vibratoing the hip ♭7th (B♭), check out how he cherry-picks the C composite blues scale in measures 1–4 (I) with the root (C), 5th (G), and jazzy 6th (A) notes—faves of the Western Swing boys back in the day of Bob Wills and the Texas Playboys in the 1940s. Dig the use of the 4th (F), however, for musical tension and the tempo-stretching hammer-on of the ♭3rd (E♭) to the major 3rd (E) across the bar line of measures 3 and 4. Over the IV (F) chord in measures 5 and 6 he allows virtually the same notes (with different phrasing) to function as the 5th (C), 3rd (A), and 2nd (G) notes. Dig again how he slides across the bar line of measures 6 and 7 with the 2nd of F to the 6th of C. Back on the I chord in measures 7 and 8 Bugs uses a combination of the root (C) with the ♭3rd (E♭) and major 3rd (E) in measure 7, and the root with the 5th (G) and 6th (A) in measure 8 to restate the basic tonality. For the V chord (G) in measure 9 he shifts up to the extension position of the C minor pentatonic scale to bend to the diatonic major 7th (F♯), finger the ♭7th (F), and run down through the ♭6th (E♭), 4th (C), and snarky ♭3rd (B♭) notes before crossing the bar line between measures 9 and 10 with the root (G) of the former measure to the root (F) of the latter. "Lounging" in measure 10 (IV), Bugs lays on the root (F) and ♭7th (E♭). Continuing with a motif begun in measure 3, he moves from the ♭7th of F one half step to the major 3rd (E) of C across the bar line of measures 10 and 11. He firmly establishes the tonality of the I chord in measure 11 with the 3rd (E), 5th (G), and 6th (A) notes, using the same notes to imply G9 via the root (G) and 9th (A) in measure 12.

TRACK 16

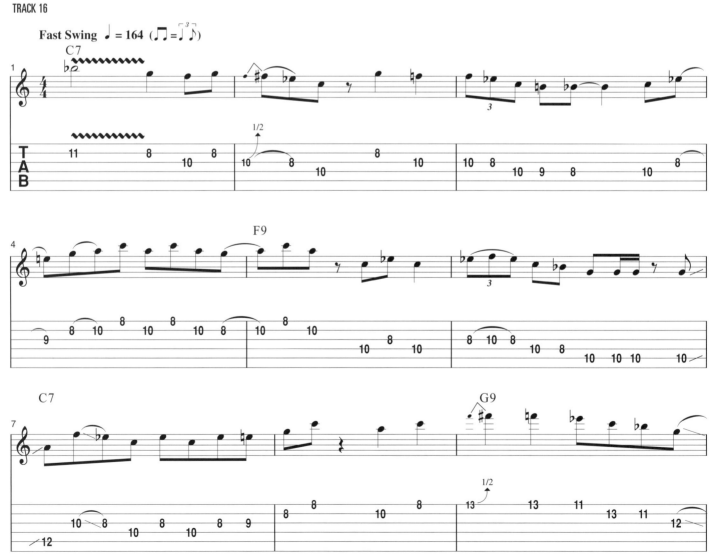

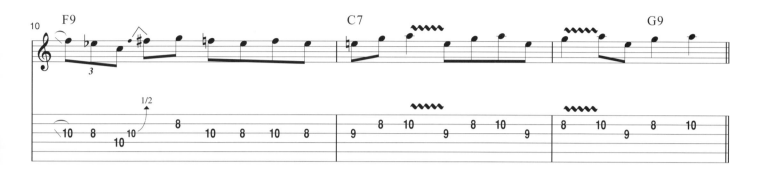

Bugs Henderson Selected Discography

American Music (Flat Canyon)

Years in the Jungle (Trigger)

Daredevils of the Red Guitar (Flat Canyon)

That's the Truth (Flat Canyon)

ALVIN LEE
Speed Kills?

It is unfortunate that his public relations people deemed it necessary to brand Alvin Lee with the questionable sobriquet of the fastest axe in the West. In fact, before he bought into the hype (and afterwards when he distanced himself from it), Lee was and is a tasty, sometimes jazzy blues-rock guitarist. Besides, if for nothing else, that he favored a red, early 1960s Gibson ES-335 (with a peace sign decal) over the now *de rigeur* Strat is almost reason enough to give him his props.

Alvin Lee was born Graham Barnes on December 19, 1944 in Wollaton Park Nottingham, England, to Sam and Doris. His father was a record collector, and Lee grew up listening to the blues of Lonnie Johnson and Big Bill Broonzy. Both parents played guitar and had a country and western trio with Lee's older sister Janice. He began playing the clarinet as a child, but in 1957 (the magic year for so many young Brits) after coming under the intoxicating spell of American pop culture via Bill Haley, Elvis, and even James Dean, he switched to the guitar. The rebellious nature of the rapidly developing teen demographic influenced Lee as well, and he was often sent home from the Margaret-Glen-Bott school for "inappropriate clothing." More than most aspiring rock 'n' rollers of his generation, Lee had the full support of his parents as was evident when he cut his fingers while working at a local metal fabricating shop and his mother told him to save his fingers for the guitar and just concentrate on his music.

Photo by Richard Aaron

Peace, brother! Alvin Lee making a "guitar face" with his early 1960s Gibson ES-335.

Lee advanced at an astonishing rate and played his first gig on guitar at the age of thirteen in 1957 with Alan Upton and the Jailbreakers. Providing the live entertainment before a Bridget Bardot film and being billed as "Alvin Lee and his Amazing Talking Guitar" was an omen for things to come "ten years after" when he would be the envy of groupies and fans of flashy guitar. His next bands were with the Top Forty combos of Vince Marshall and the Square Caps followed by Ivan Jay and the Jaycats. In 1961 Lee met bassist Leo Lyons, who would become his long-time musical partner, around the same time that Ivan Jay split, leaving Lee to take over on guitar and vocals. As the newly dubbed Jaycats, Lee and Lyons took the band to Hamburg, Germany and followed the Beatles into the famous Star Club. Located in the infamous red light district known as Reeperbahn, the month-long gig exposed the seventeen-year old to the requisite "sex, drugs, and rock 'n' roll."

When they returned to the U.K. the Jaycats backed visiting American groups like the Drifters and continued making forays back to Hamburg. Between 1962–66 they remained in Nottingham as their base of operations, trim-ming the band down to a blues power trio with newly hired drummer Ric Lee. In 1966 they finally made the big move to London and its very competitive music scene and added Chick Churchill on Hammond B-3 organ. They scuffled for a while recording demos for a publisher and as the backing band for a stage play starring Albert Finney before hooking up with a high-powered agent and manager named

Chris Wright. They changed their name to the much hipper Ten Years After—a reference to the preceding period of rock and blues that inspired them—and Wright snared them a contract with Deram Records, a subsidiary of Decca. A single, "Love Like A Man" was released (and re-recorded on *Cricklewood Green* in 1970), becoming their only hit (#20) in Great Britain, while their debut album *Ten Years After* came out in 1967 followed by *Undead* and *Stonedhenge* (with the frantic and ominously-titled "Speed Kills") in 1968. Before the emergence of Led Zeppelin, Ten Years After was the biggest-selling rock band in the British Isles, and in June of 1968 they toured the U.S., for the first of *50* subsequent Stateside forays, at the behest of Fillmore promoter Bill Graham.

Ssssh from 1969 was a musical and critical highpoint (#6 in the U.K.) for the band with the epic, leering version of "Good Morning Little Schoolgirl" ("Baby, want to ball you"), but the true turning point came when TYA appeared at the Woodstock Festival in August. Lee's orgiastic rock 'n' roll boogie "Goin' Home" was prominently featured in the motion picture chronicling the watershed counterculture event, and he was instantly turned into a golden-tressed rock god. Though basically nine minutes of pull-offs and triplets strung together, Lee's sense of dynamics and drama elevated the track to iconic status even as it helped to spell the end of the self-indulgent, wanking guitar solo in the 1970s.

TYA was always the Alvin Lee show (as 1972's *Alvin Lee & Co.* attests), but in the 1970s he became a virtuosic parody playing to the choir, as well as becoming a serious substance abuser. *A Space in Time* (1971), however, showed a willingness to go in more of a pop direction with the single "I'd Love to Change the World" reaching #40. The band stayed together until 1974, but he started recording solo projects in 1973 with *On the Road to Freedom*. *In Flight* was released in 1974 followed by *Pump Iron* in 1975. Going for broke, Lee put together another power trio with Tom Compton (drums) and Mick Hawksworth (bass) in 1978 called, wittily enough, *Ten Years Later,* and they released *Rocket Fuel* followed by *Ride On* in 1979. Changing course again, Lee commenced the Alvin Lee Band for *Free Fall* (1980) and *RX5* (1981), after which the word "band" was dropped from the group name and ex-Stones guitarist Mick Taylor was brought into the fold for a short stint. By this time Lee had come to grips with his drug demons and regained his health.

After a five-year hiatus Lee returned with the harder rocking *Detroit Diesel* in 1986, but the bigger news was a TYA reunion in 1989. After they recorded *About Time* Lee went back to his solo career, releasing *Zoom* (1992) and *I Hear You Rockin'* (1994), a surprising return to his "roots" with *Pure Blues* (1995) and then *Live in Vienna* (1996). TYA was reconvened for yet another reunion tour in 1997, and a TYA anthology, *Solid Rock*, was released later in the year. The successful tour encouraged Lee to have another go with his old mates in 1998 and 1999 as well, while also performing with his Alvin Lee band.

Alvin Lee, for better or worse, has brought his particular slant on blues guitar to light for nearly forty years. A driven musician who seems to live for the road, he once summed up his performing philosophy to writer Peter Frame as such: "I never want to stop being a working musician. I look at Muddy Waters and John Lee Hooker and say to myself, 'Yeah, they are still at it… and that's the life for me as well.' Now I've decided that touring is the natural life for me… and I intend doing it when I'm forty or fifty years old." At the age of fifty-nine Lee has already reached his goal while adding luster to it as each year goes passing by.

The Blues Guitar Style of Alvin Lee

Alvin Lee's idea of blues is… the faster the better! He will play a sixteenth note where an eighth note would do, and a thirty-second note where a sixteenth note would do. That said, he can move with breathtaking rapidity up and down the fingerboard, a characteristic that has a proud tradition extending back to Auburn "Pat" Hare and Lafayette "Thing" Thomas in the 1950s. As previously mentioned, a big red, early 1960s Gibson ES-335, with a Fender single coil pickup custom-installed in between the two humbuckers, has been his trademark speed machine.

In Track 17 Alvin locks his hand into the twelfth position of the E blues scale (with brief forays up to the extension position) and rips a slow blues from end to end. Though he once recorded an album called *Rocket Fuel,* his approach to the changes is not "rocket science." Basically, he emphasizes the root notes. Embracing these notes are dynamic runs up and down the scale that sometimes bridge two measures, as in measures 7 and 8. Alvin also creates musical tension by bending, as in measure 3 where he raises the ♭3rd (G) to the 4th (A) before resolving back to the root (E) note. Another of his dynamic phrasing devices is to begin a measure with a sustained and vibratoed quarter note (A = the 4th in measure 8, G = the blues-approved ♭3rd in measure 2, G = the ♭7th of IV (A) in measure 6, and B = the root in measure 9). In measures 11 and 12 (turnaround) he maintains his established procedure with the root notes.

TRACK 17   **Slow Blues** ♩ = 72 (♫ = ♩ ♪)

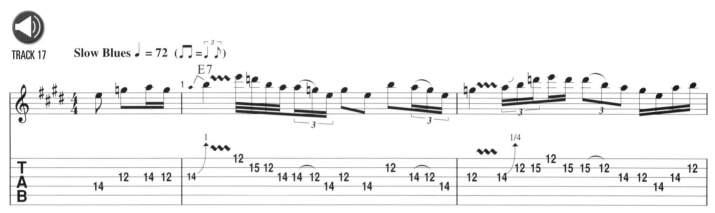

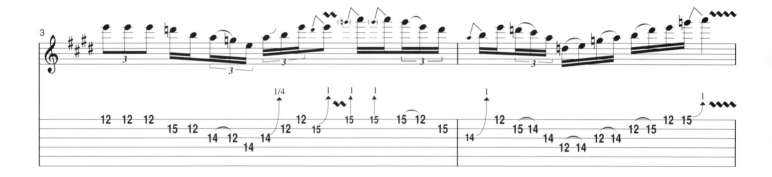

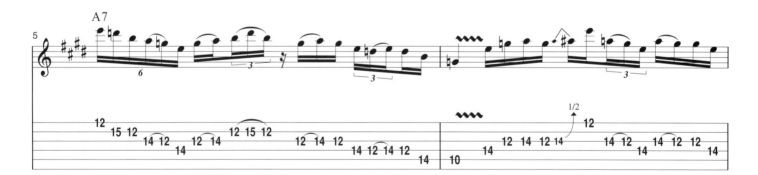

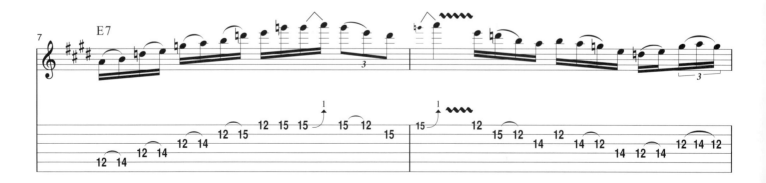

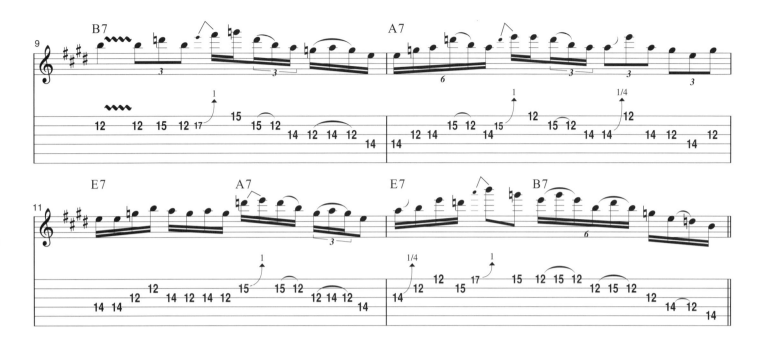

Track 18 shows some of the crowd-pleasing, repeating patterns that Alvin plays in songs such as his rock 'n' roll extravaganza "Goin' Home." In measures 1–4 (I) he establishes the tonality with a sixteenth-note riff of the bluesy hammer from the ♭3rd (C) to the major 3rd (C♯) followed by the 5th (E) hammered to the 6th (F♯). The inclusion of the 6th is a tasty touch reminiscent of swing jazz and rockabilly. The six-note phrase in measures 5 and 6 over the IV chord (D) is a staple (one might say cliché) of British blues-rock that highlights the ♭7th (C), 5th (A), 6th (B), and 3rd (F♯) notes from the D Mixolydian mode. Thundering dyads drive measures 7 and 8 (I) (G/E = ♭7th and 5th), measure 9 (V) (C♯/G♯ = 6th and 3rd), and measure 10 (IV) (B/F♯ = 6th and 3rd). Dig that the dyads for the IV and V chord changes are not the typical 3rds but a more sophisticated double-stop variety as found in jazz, western swing, and rockabilly music. Alvin closes out his powerful chorus with rippling pull-offs derived from the A Dorian mode that keep the relentless momentum flowing through measures 11 and 12 and emphasize the root (A) and 5th (E) notes.

Performance Tip: For the six-note riff in measures 5 and 6 use strict alternate down and up picking. For the screaming dyads in measures 7–10 also use alternating down and up pick strokes for efficiency (and to keep your wrist from falling off!). In measures 11 and 12, use an upstroke on string 1 and a downstroke on string 2 to begin the double pull-offs that follow, respectively.

Fast Rock
TRACK 18   **Double-time feel** ♩ = 106

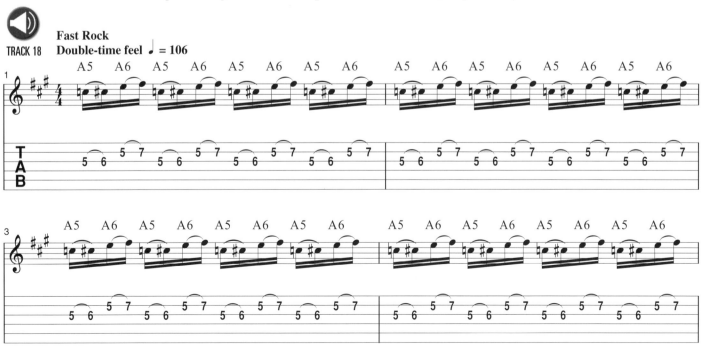

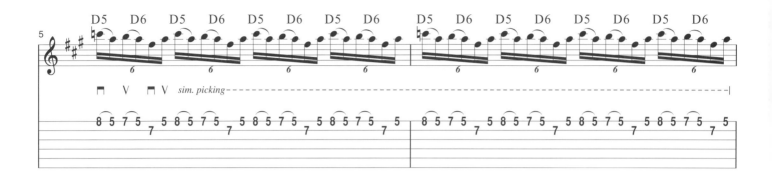

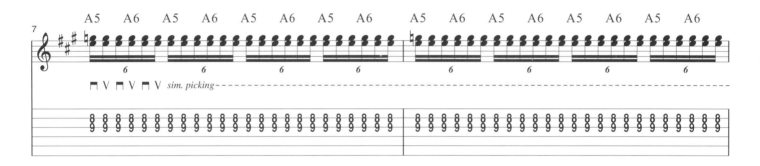

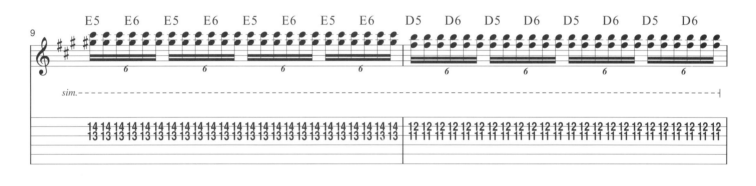

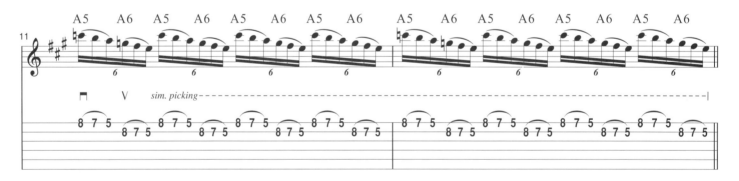

Alvin Lee Selected Discography

With Ten Years After:

Ten Years After (Polygram)

Undead (Deram)

Sssh (EMI-Capitol)

Stonedhenge (Beat Goes On)

Live at the Fillmore East (Capitol)

Photo by Neil Zlozower

Have another Miller: Steve "flies like an eagle" on an Ibanez Iceman.

STEVE MILLER
Take the Money and Run

Virtually all blues-rock guitarists have succumbed, to some degree, to the siren-like lure of the commercial music world. Stevie "Guitar" Miller heeded the call more than most and has benefitted handsomely from the crossover. An exceedingly talented and authentic blues guitarist when the spirit moves him, he proved even more adept at crafting catchy pop-rock tunes based on common rock and blues conventions.

Steve Miller was born on October 5, 1943 in Milwaukee, Wisconsin. His father, Dr. George "Sonny" Miller, was a pathologist who also happened to be an amateur recording engineer. The Millers were a musical family, and young Steve started playing guitar when he was four years old. The good doctor was friends with many musicians like Charles Mingus and Les Paul, who was a regular visitor to the Miller household and showed five-year old Steve his first chords; Les even once allowed him to attend a recording session. A mutual fascination with recording technology was certainly a factor in their relationship, and Dr. Miller was best man at the wedding of Les Paul and Mary Ford on December 29, 1949.

In 1950 the Miller family relocated to Dallas, Texas, and the circle of musicians who dropped by the old homestead was expanded to include T-Bone Walker while the doctor continued recording his favorite music. Steve formed his first band, the Marksmen, when he was twelve, and received considerable on-the-job training when the rock 'n' roll combo was booked playing college fraternities. The band lasted for five years, and when Steve reached high school he invited his buddy William Royce "Boz" Scaggs in to sing. At the age of sixteen in 1959, Miller effectively broke up the band by going off to college in Wisconsin, but not before he and Scaggs received the thrill of their lifetime by backing up blues legend Jimmy Reed. At the University of Wisconsin in Madison, Miller formed the Ardells. He taught Scaggs some chords on the guitar during summer vacation after his freshman year, and they returned to Madison together the following year to continue on with the Ardells. The following summer Miller remained in Madison and played with the Knightranes. During Miller's junior year in 1961 Ben Sidran joined the band on keyboards.

Miller spent a semester during his senior year at the University of Denmark, but instead of returning to Madison or Dallas for the summer, he opted to go to Chicago in 1964. He immersed himself in the flourishing blues scene and was afforded the opportunity to play with a young, up-and-coming harmonica cat named Paul Butterfield. Just shy a few credits from graduating, Miller moved to Chi-town for the blues experience and was soon jamming and receiving encouragement from Buddy Guy, Muddy Waters, and Howlin' Wolf. In time he met organist Barry Goldberg, bassist Roy Ruby (a close friend of Mike Bloomfield), and drummer Maurice McKinley, and formed the Goldberg-Miller Blues Band. They were signed to Epic Records and cut a precious few tracks, while also appearing on the pop TV music show *Hullabaloo* with the Supremes and the Four Tops. A steady club gig in Manhattan lasted a short while, and when the band returned to Chicago they were welcomed back to a moribund blues scene.

Discouraged from his brief fling with trying to be a professional blues musician, Miller went home to Texas with the hopes of studying music at the University of Texas in Austin. In the interim he worked as a janitor at the college while composing songs that would eventually end up on his first album. Upon getting turned down for admission he decided to head west to San Francisco in 1966 in a VW Microbus for the start of the flowering counterculture movement. Despite coming from a wealthy family, Miller was likely on his own at this point since failing to complete college, as he supposedly spent his last few bucks to catch the Paul Butterfield Blues Band and the Jefferson Airplane at the Fillmore West. Jamming with Butterfield convinced him to make "Mean Old 'Frisco" his home. Miller then found drummer Tim Davis, an acquaintance from back in Madison, and with guitarist James "Curley" Cooke and bassist Lonnie Turner, the Steve Miller Blues Band was born. Attesting to his destitution, Miller slept in his van until the band started gigging regularly at the Avalon Ballroom and Fillmore West in 1967, leading to a plum opportunity at the landmark Monterey Pop Festival in June. Things moved quickly from there as the SMBB backed up Chuck Berry at the Fillmore a week later (presciently recorded for posterity) and were shortly thereafter signed to Capitol Records. Never one to be shy about his talents or worth, Miller was able to negotiate a "record-breaking" contract. He brought in his old pal Boz Scaggs on guitar, keyboardist Jim Peterman replaced Cooke, the word "blues" was excised from the band name, and they split for England in 1968 to cut their debut, *Children of the Future*. An instant FM radio fave, it was followed later in the same year by *Sailor* (#24) which yielded the single "Living in the U.S.A" (#94) and Miller's cover of the old Johnny "Guitar" Watson classic, "Gangster of Love." The cover tune choice was significant as it introduced the first of Miller's assumed personas. Meanwhile, Peterman left to be replaced by Ben Sidran, and Scaggs opted out for a solo career as the Steve Miller Band continued with its winning combination of blue-based rock dosed with a hit of experimental psychedelia.

Brave New World (# 22) followed in 1969 with "Space Cowboy," another adopted guise for Miller. Mixed in England by Miller and Glyn Johns, it provided him the opportunity for a meeting with Paul McCartney, who played bass and drums on "My Dark Hour" under the pseudonym of Paul Ramon. Quickly building momentum as a hip, underground favorite, the Steve Miller Band also released *Your Saving Grace* (#38) and *Revolution* in 1969. Additionally, Miller was involved in a number of outside projects resulting in bitter feeling among the band members. Turner and Sidran left, and Miller headed to Nashville with unfinished tapes and enlisted top session guys to finish *Number 5* in 1970. Unbeknownst at the time, it would signal the end of the first artistic period of Steve Miller as the rhythm section took their leave. *Rock Love*, a live album of blues-rock clichés was released in 1971 to virtually no acclaim.

Recall the Beginning... A Journey from Eden followed in 1972 with yet another alter ego for Miller: "Maurice" and the "pompitous of love" on the appropriately titled "Enter Maurice." Though not planned as such, it would be the transition album to Miller's greatest commercial success that would blast him to superstardom in the mid-1970s. Unfortunately, fate played a role in the process, however, as Miller was seriously injured in a car accident in 1972 while on the way to the airport to begin a tour of Europe. His neck was broken, he contracted hepatitis, and he returned to his parents' home in Dallas for an eight-month recuperation. While recovering he took inventory of his career to date and contemplated major changes in his music.

Upon his recovery he headed back to California in 1973, and with new band mates produced and completed *The Joker* in a brisk nineteen days. The album went to #2, the title track became Miller's first #1, and "Your Cash Ain't Nothin' But Trash" managed to reach #51. Critically the album was "trashed," as many complained about its blatantly derivative and mediocre nature. Nonetheless, Miller began playing arenas instead of theaters while acts like Boz Scaggs and blues harmonica legend James Cotton began opening for him. After a hectic five years of recording and touring he decided to take the next year and a half off to write and record his next two albums in his home studio on the farm he had recently purchased. *Fly Like an Eagle* was released in 1976 and hit #3 with the title track clocking in at #2. "Rock N' Me," though reminiscent of Free's "Alright Now," among other classic rockers, zoomed to #1. The ironically titled "Take the Money and Run" sprinted to #11, and Miller was established as an arena rock monster. The unrepentant Space Cowboy followed with *Book of Dreams* in 1977 and continued the breathless pace by topping out at #2 with Paul Pena's "Jet Airliner" (with Clapton's "Crossroads" lick grafted on) soaring to #8, "Swingtown" dancing to #17, and "Jungle Love" roaring to #23.

Taking another hiatus at the peak of his popularity, Miller resurfaced in 1981 with the disappointing *Circle of Love*. With one entire side filled up with "Macho Blues" (Space Cowboy, indeed!) and no catchy pop hits on the order of the previous two quadruple platinum platters, it may have looked like the "Gangster of Love" had been busted. Not one to be counted out so easily, however, he came back for one more shot of glory with *Abracadabra* in 1982. His lightest and silliest pop foray to date, it still materialized at #3 with the title track appearing at #4. In addition, "Give It Up" came in at #60 a year later.

Alas, the great ten-year run to reap the commercial harvest had come to an end. A live album was released in 1983 that encapsulated the recent hits, and *Italian X Rays* came out a year later. It did not even crack the Top 100, let alone the Top 10 like the previous albums, though the singles "Shangri-La" (#57) and "Bongo Bongo" (#84) charted. *Living in the 20th Century* from 1987 faired better at #65, while the single "I Want to Turn the World Around" (featuring Kenny G!) eked into the Top 100 at #97 while hitting #1 on the Mainstream Rock Tracks. A good measure of the relative success of the LP must go to the number of good blues covers included on side two. The misleadingly-titled *Born 2B Blue* from 1988 was actually a collection of laid-back jazz covers that garnered credibility with guest spots from saxist Phil Woods and vibraphonist Milt Jackson. The same year his old friend Les Paul invited Miller to appear with other guitar luminaries in a Cinemax special called *Les Paul and Friends*, and the experience inspired him to go back on the road for the first time since the tours to support *Abracadabra* in 1982.

Wide River in 1993 was Miller's last studio album of new material and was a deliberate attempt to recapture the pop-rock sound of the mid-1970s that had been so wildly successful. The album placed a respectable #85, and the title track reached #64 as a single. Since then he has toured regularly while enjoying a nice return on his albums to the tune of a million plus sales a year.

The Blues Guitar Style of Steve Miller

Say what you will about the man's Top 40 music, but when Steve Miller plays the blues he digs into the electric roots of the genre and expresses deep feeling with authentic, muscular phrasing powered by his considerable chops. Given his lifelong friendship with Les Paul, it is only natural that he has played the master's namesake axe as well as the regulation-required Strats.

Track 19 exhibits his syncopated lines to good effect in a moody slow blues. Using the basic 12th fretposition of the E blues scale in eleven of the twelve measures, Steve extracts maximum variety out of the restricted note palette. Check out his employment of the D (♭7th of I, 4th of IV) bent one step to the E (root of I, 5th of IV) as a motif sustained across the bar line in the pickup and measures 1–4. As a dynamic he contrasts the high E with the one an octave lower on string 4 at fret 14 to keep the tonality centered as either the root (measures 1, 3, and 4 over the E chord) or the 5th (measure 2 over the A chord). In measures 5 and 6 (IV) he leans a little harder on the ♭7th (G) on string 3 at fret 12 and on string 5 at fret 10 for more contrast. Measure 7 (I) is the "red herring" of the bunch where Steve relocates to the seventh fret and repeats the 5th (B) and ♭7th (D) notes in order to break the predictability of the established timbre returned to in measure 8. Over the V chord (B) in measure 9 he acknowledges the root (B) while staying within the confines of the 4th (E), ♭7th (A), and the garlicky ♭3rd (D) and ♭6th (G) notes. The root (A) is emphasized in measure 10 over the IV chord while Steve ends where he began his "journey to the blues" by repeating the ♭7th (D) bent to the root (E) in measure 12 for uncontested resolution. Dig the half-step bend from the ♭3rd (G) to the major 3rd (G♯) in measure 12 and the logical use of the root (B) notes on beats 3 and 4 of the V chord.

Performance Tip: In measure 1 pull down on the G note with your index finger and bend up on the ♭7th (D) with your pinky (backed up by the ring, middle, and index fingers) on beats 3 and 4, respectively.

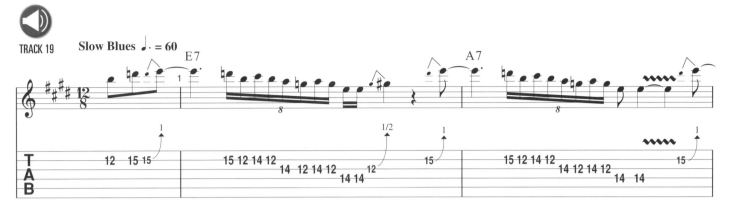

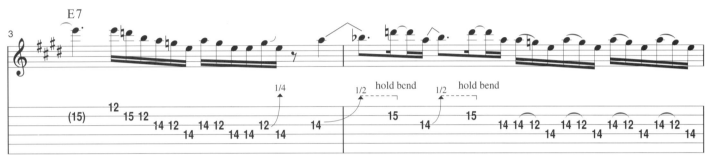

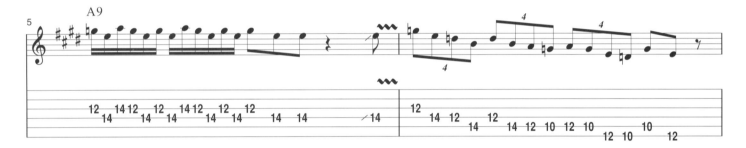

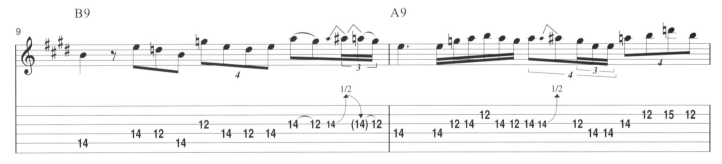

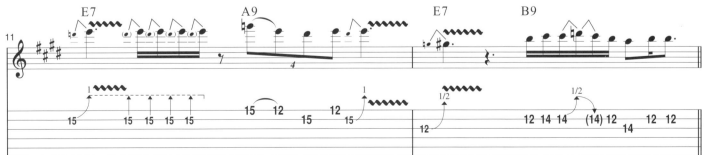

Steve takes a much different approach in the modal, uptempo "John Lee Hooker" boogie of Track 20 in the key of A. In measures 1–6 he mines the "B.B. King box" for blues nuggets. In measures 7–12 he moves on up to the less-explored blues box at fret 12 where, in measures 8, 9, and 12, particularly, he rapidly alternates the root with the ♭3rd and 4th for exciting musical tension and energy.

Performance Tip: To access the dyad in measure 10 efficiently, bend the 4th (D) up with your ring finger (backed up by the middle and index fingers) while holding down the ♭7th (G) with your pinky.

Steve Miller Selected Discography

Sailor (Alliance)

Number 5 (Capitol)

Rock Love (Capitol)

Living in the 20th Century (EMI-Capitol)

Stairway to the blues: Jimmy Page piloting the Zep with a vintage Gibson Les Paul 'Burst.

JIMMY PAGE
Whole Lotta Blues

The magical, mythical, mystical (not to mention foot-tapping) combination of blues and rock has proved to be a bottomless source of inspiration for artistic and commercial success since at least the early 1950s with Bill Haley and Chuck Berry. Many great guitarists have arisen from the genre as demonstrated by the fiery artists covered in this book. Far and away (if not over the hills) the most accomplished blues-rock guitarist of all time would have to be Jimmy Page, however. Exceptionally facile, with an unparalleled ear for tone and a knack for turning blues cliches into riff rock gold, he has left a recorded legacy (hopefully not finished!) that will surely continue to inspire aspiring rock heroes who hear "Heartbreaker" for the first time.

James Patrick Page was born on January 9, 1944 in Heston, Middlesex, England to an industrial personnel officer and a doctor's secretary. After a period of time spent on his uncle's farm in Northamtonshire they relocated to Epsom, Surrey, where Page attended Epsom Grammar School. His first musical experience occurred in the school choir as he also showed artistic and athletic (!) ability as a champion hurdler. At the age of thirteen, in that once again significant British blues year of 1957, his parents gave him an acoustic flattop guitar and, again like his peers, he became totally obsessed with it. He was basically self-taught and played constantly, including in school where he often had his axe taken away when he dared to practice in class. The rock 'n' roll bug did not bite, however, until he heard Scotty Moore's magnificent rockabilly guitar on Elvis' "Baby, Let's Play House" on the album *A Date with Elvis* in 1959. Along with Moore's appealing style, Page copped licks from an eclectic mix including James Burton, Johnny Day (the Everly Brothers sideman along with Chet Atkins), Elmore James, B.B. King, Bert Jansch, and John Renbourn.

At fifteen in 1959 he left school and tried getting a day job as a laboratory assistant. Failing that, he scored his first musical gig backing beat poet Robert Ellis with guitar accompaniment at his readings. In addition, he also played with bluesman Red E. Lewis. Neil Christian caught one of his performances in a dancehall and invited him to join his Crusaders. Christian sang pop along with Bo Diddley and Chuck Berry covers, and Page went out on the road for the first time. Unfortunately, his constitution was not up to the rigors of long term, low-budget touring, and he eventually contracted glandular fever, ending his two-year membership in the band. Leaving for a period of recuperation, Page contemplated forgoing a musical career and entered Croydon Art College where he pursued painting until mid-1963. He continued to play, however, jamming with friends including Jeff Beck, whom he had met in 1955.

The startling success of the Rolling Stones with classic American blues and R&B music in the early 1960s piqued Page's musical muse again. While still studying art he began sitting in with R&B and jazz groups at the Crawdaddy Club in Richmond, the Marquee in London, and at Eel Pie Island in Twickenham. During one jam session with the Cyril Davies All-Stars at the Marquee, producer Mike Leander approached him about playing on a planned single for two former members of Hank Marvin's Shadows (and Cliff Richards' backup band), Tony Meehan (drums) and Jet Harris (bass). With future Zep engineer Glyn Johns manning the board, Page was relegated to playing rhythm, as he could not read the sheet music placed in front of him. A few quick lessons with a Kingston-On-Thames teacher set him on the path to rudimentary reading and writing, however, and "Diamonds," an instrumental reminiscent of Duane Eddy and recorded in January 1963, shone all the way to #1 in the U.K.

The surprising success of his first record as a studio guitarist made Page an instant, in-demand studio cat. From early 1963 until the middle of 1966 when he followed Jeff Beck into the Yardbirds, he was the darling of producers Leander, Andrew Loog Oldham, Mickie Most, Shel Tamy, and Bert Berns. After a brief fling with Mickie Finn and the Blue Men as a harp player (!), starting in early 1964 Page was averaging ten pop and rock sessions a week. Though there are many questions relating to the exact sessions, it is generally accepted that he backed up The Who ("Bald-Headed Woman," the B side of "I Can't Explain"), the Kinks (first LP, but probably not the solo on "You Really Got Me" as long rumored), Jackie DeShannon (with whom he shared a romance), The Pretty Things, the Nashville Teens ("Tobacco Road"), Brenda Lee, Lulu, Joe Cocker, Marianne Faithful, Herman's Hermits, Tom Jones ("It's Not Unusual"), and Donovan, among many others. He also recorded an exceedingly rare single in February of 1965 under his own name, "She Satisfies" b/w "Keep Moving," featuring his guitar and *vocals* that unfortunately stiffed. The same year he contributed to a series of blues jam sessions with Jeff Beck and Eric Clapton on the Immediate label for producer Oldham (of Rolling Stones fame). A busy year for "Pagey," 1965 was also when he received his first offer to join the Yardbirds when Clapton decided to leave. Content with the relative financial security of session work and afraid of offending Clapton by looking like an opportunist, he declined and recommended his buddy Jeff Beck.

In June of 1966, however, Yardbirds bassist Paul Samwell-Smith decided to hang it up, and Beck talked Page into covering on bass until rhythm guitarist Chris Dreja could learn the instrument (though neither had any experience with it) with the idea of eventually receiving the unprecedented opportunity to perform in a dual guitar lineup. In fact, some time would pass before Dreja was ready, and session bassists were called in to record so that Page and Beck could engage in what was, for too short a time, a rock guitar freak's fantasy come true. On "Happenings Ten Years Time Ago" (the only official studio track with both guitar gods) John Paul Jones handled the bass chores in a tantalizing preview of what would occur in 1968. Before that, the Beck/Page tandem also appeared in Italian movie director Michaelangelo Antonioni's mod classic *Blow Up* in October, 1968, miming to a version of "The Train Kept A-Rollin'" retitled "Stroll On." In November Beck quit the Yardbirds while they were on tour in the U.S.

Page stayed on with Dreja through the recording of *Little Games* in April 1967 with Jones on bass and the debut of his famous violin bowing technique on "Puzzles." Though the songwriting and production was wildly uneven in this period, Page took the Yardbirds further into psychedelia and experimentation than had occurred even during Beck's relatively short tenure. Tours and more singles followed, but on July 7, 1968, the "original Yardbirds" played their last gig. Singer Keith Relf and drummer Jim McCarty were anxious to move on with a new pop project, while Page and Dreja were willing to go on and play the band's remaining bookings. Robert Plant was brought in to sing, and he in turn recommended drummer John Bonham. A devious trick was played on Chris Dreja, one of the founders of the group with McCarty, and he was aced out in favor of John Paul Jones, despite his co-ownership of the band name with McCarty! Much acrimony occurred over Page, Plant, Jones, and Bonham going out as the Yardbirds after the contractual obligations for the band had been fulfilled, but it became moot when the name change to Led Zeppelin was officially reported in the rock press on October 18, 1968. Though the late Who drummer Keith Moon has been credited with coining the name, the late Who bassist John Entwistle always maintained that he was the one that said the group assembled for "Beck's Bolero" was "going down like a lead zeppelin" (The spelling of the first part of the name was changed to avoid it being pronounced as "leed"). Their first gig was November 9, 1968.

The mighty Zep, instead of going down in flames like the Hindenburg as depicted on the cover of their debut album in 1969, soared to heights undreamed of by the Yardbirds or Clapton's blues-rock supergroup Cream, until 1980. From the two Willie Dixon-penned classics on the debut album, "You Shook Me" and "I Can't Quit You, Baby" to Memphis Minnie's "When the Levee Breaks" on the "Stairway to Heaven"-dominated *Led Zeppelin IV* to the epic, original slow blues, "Since I've Been Loving You" on *Led Zeppelin III*, and others, Page has demonstrated his uncanny affinity for the form.

When John Bonham overdosed on alcohol on September 25, 1980 and died at the age of thirty-three, Page was so distraught that Zeppelin deflated, and he entered a two-year period where he hardly played, while nursing the heroin habit he had acquired in the late 1970s. In 1982 he surfaced to contribute music to the soundtracks of *Death Wish I* and *II*, received a twelve-month conditional discharge for drug-related offenses, and joined his old mates Beck and Clapton for the A.R.M.S. tour for multiple sclerosis in 1983. In 1984 he combined forces with former Free and Bad Company vocalist Paul Rodgers in the Firm, but they dissolved the partnership after two albums. With drummers Phil Collins and Tony Thompson, Page, Plant, and Jones reunited for Live Aid in Philadelphia in 1985, but the rock guitar legend turned in a shabby performance. Three years later the band came together again with Bonham's son Jason behind the trap kit for the Atlantic Records 25th Anniversary Concert at Madison Square Garden, but the results were woefully the same. Undaunted, Page played on Plant's solo effort *Now & Zen* and released his own solo debut, *Outrider*.

When Plant refused to reunite Zeppelin a few years later, Page convened the Coverdale/Page band with former Deep Purple singer David Coverdale, and they kept it together for only one album in 1993. A year later Plant relented and joined Page (Jones was inexplicably left out) for the acoustic *No Quarter* and the similar *MTV Unplugged*, followed by a smash, sold out world tour. In 1995 Led Zeppelin was inducted into the Rock and Roll Hall of Fame in an encore appearance for Page who had previously strolled in with the Yardbirds in 1992. Page and Plant released *Walking into Clarksdale* in 1998 to little interest, and the longtime collaborators called it a day. Page joined the Black Crowes for a tour and a live album, *Live at the Greek*, in 2000, though a second tour was torpedoed when Page hurt his back. In 2001, however, he joined Plant on stage to celebrate the sixtieth birthday of folk artist Roy Harper. To the wildly enthusiastic response of Zeppelin's countless fans, in 2003 Page oversaw the release of separate DVD and CD box sets with previously unreleased live performances.

The Blues Guitar Style of Jimmy Page

How an English lad given to excessive debauchery and who appears to express himself so inadequately in print can be so lyrical and eloquent when negotiating 12-bar changes is a mystery. One answer may be the seeming lack of inhibition and freewheeling (some would say "sloppy," but this is a canard) approach Jimmy Page brings to the blues and all his best rock music, for that matter. Maybe he has actually managed to channel Otis Rush the same as his attempts with Aleister Crowley! Whatever his secret, he has turned vintage Les Paul 'bursts into magic wands enough times to cast a permanent spell over his multitude of fans and erstwhile imitators.

Track 21 is a slinky slow blues that Jimmy negotiates via the A composite blues scale (blues scale plus Mixolydian mode) and its offshoot, the F# blues scale (relative minor to A major). He begins in measure 1 with an ascending run that starts on the 6th (F#) and ends on the root (A), combining notes from both scales for his dynamic chorus of blues. In measure 2 he accesses the major 3rd (C#) and minor 3rd (C) from the 4th (D) in an unusual move on beats 1 and 2. Measures 3 and 4 contain a series of bends that really propels the I chord to the IV (D). In measure 3 Jimmy applies leverage to the root (A) note, lifting it up to the ♭3rd (C) for tension before going up through the "B.B. King box" around fret 10 to the 5th (E). Without missing a "beat" (pun intended!) he starts right in on whipping the 5th up one step to the 6th (F#), one half step to the ♭6th, one and one-half steps to the ♭7th (G), and then a bluesy quarter step before further setting up the IV chord change with the ♭3rd (C)—the ♭7th leading to D. Jimmy keeps the pressure (and tension) on in measures 5 and 6 over the IV chord by studiously avoiding the root (D) while bending the ♭7th (C) to the ♭9th (E♭) and the 9th (E), punctuating his point with the root (D) bent up one step to the 9th on beat 4 of measure 6. In measures 7 and 8 (I) he plays a similar run to measure 1 (using the A major pentatonic scale in second position), resolving to the root (finally!) on beat 1 of measure 8. Another series of bends off the root, similar to measure 3, in the "Albert King box" is capped with the sweet 3rd (C#) on beat 4. Jimmy then focuses on the pivotal measure 9 (V = E) with the 9th (F#), root (E), and musically abrasive ♭6th (C) phrased in snappy sixteenth notes, but satisfactorily resolves to the sustained and vibratoed root on beat 4. Maintaining the momentum, he repeats the 9th (E) and 4th (G) notes in measure 10 over the IV chord (D) before outlining the turnaround in measures 11 and 12 with the root (A) for the I, the 4th and 9th (G/E) again for the IV, the root for the I, and the root (E) for the V following a traditional run down the A blues scale at the 5th fret.

TRACK 21

Slow Blues ♩ = 60

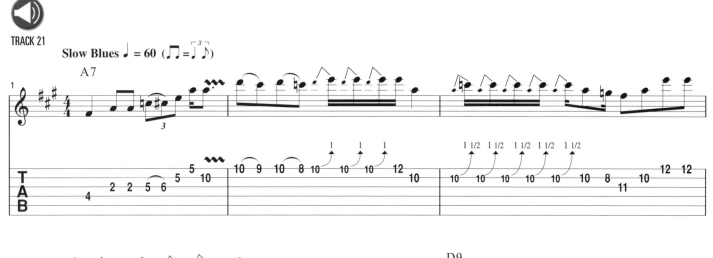

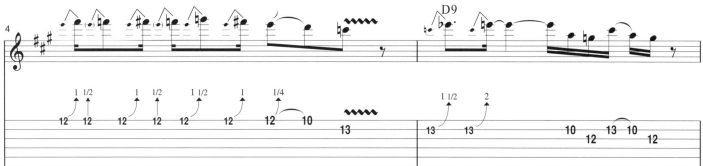

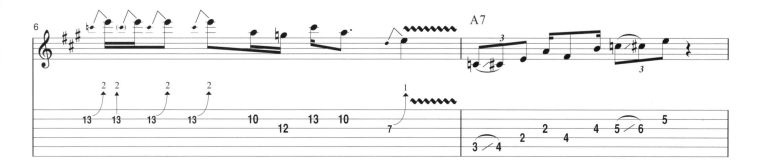

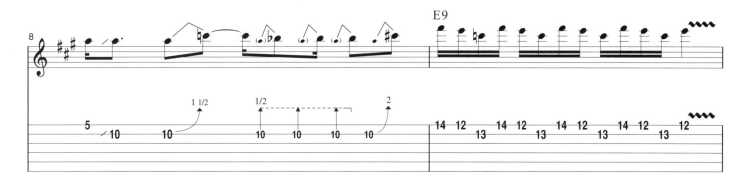

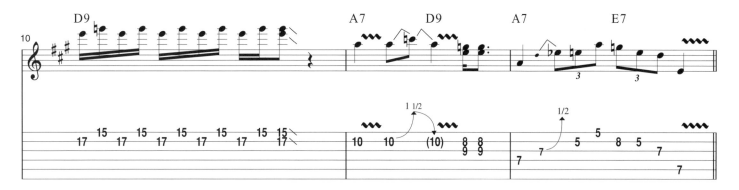

Jimmy also uses the A composite blues scale and F♯ relative minor pentatonic scale to propel a fast boogie blues in Track 22. Dig how he uses musical rests throughout to intensify the explosive quality of his hot licks. In measures 1 and 2 in the basic 5th-fret position of the A blues scale he acknowledges his Chicago blues roots with the classic bend of the 4th (D) to the 5th (E), released and pulled off to the ♭3rd (C) and resolving to the root (A). Starting in measures 3 and 4, however, he zeroes in mostly on string 2 in the same position with emphasis on the ♭7th (G) and 5th (E). In measures 5 and 6 over the IV chord (D) Jimmy shifts up to strings 2 and 1, where the ♭7th (C), 9th (E), 5th (A), 6th (B), and tonality-defining major 3rd (F♯) notes amplify the D chord change. He keeps the concept going on beat 1 of measure 7 of the I chord, but then repeats the bend/release lick from measure 1—though he ends the lick and the measure on the raw ♭3rd (C) for tension.

In measure 8 he conclusively resolves to the root (A), but not before playing the blues-affirming ♭7th (G) and the sweet 2nd (B) notes in combination on beats 1 and 2. Ever cognizant of the important V (E) chord change in measure 9, Jimmy shoots down to the F♯ relative minor pentatonic scale at fret 2 with heavy emphasis on the root (E) notes embellished by the 2nd (F♯) and gritty ♭3rd (G). He adjusts his hand position slightly to include the A composite blues scale in measure 10 on the IV chord with the 6th (B), ♭7th (C), ♭5th (A♭), 4th (G), 2nd (E), and major 3rd (F♯) notes. He then lands squarely in the fifth position of the A composite blues scale where he pays strict attention to the root (A), 3rd (C♯), and 5th (E) triadic tones for rock solid resolution in measure 11. In measure 12 he flies down the scale (with the hip inclusion of the ♭5th, E♭) after bending up to and sustaining the root of the V chord (E), ending on the same scale degree an octave lower on beat 4.

Performance Tip: Though Jimmy can be as much of a "three-finger" blues guitarist as his contemporary Eric Clapton, it is recommended that you use your index, ring, and pinky fingers in measures 5, 7, 9, and 12 where there are occasions of three notes on one string.

TRACK 22

Jimmy Page Selected Discography

Led Zeppelin (Atlantic)

Led Zeppelin II (Atlantic)

Led Zeppelin III (Atlantic)

Led Zeppelin IV (Atlantic)

Keith Richards showing no "Sympathy for the Devil" as he awaits his turn to start rocking on his mid-1950s Gibson Les Paul with P-90 pickups.

KEITH RICHARDS
A Rolling Stone Gathers No Moss

Chuck Berry in the 1950s and Keith Richards in the 1960s: the two most influential rock guitarists of their respective eras, masters of rhythm and the riff, and stone blues players. Not coincidentally, Richards is Berry's number one acolyte and his greatest fan. As the Rolling Stones developed relatively outside the inner circle of the blues scene in London in the early 1960s, so too did Richards. He went directly to the deep Delta blues of Muddy Waters where the *groove* and *feel* is the deal, as opposed to the instrumental virtuosity that Clapton, Green, Beck, and Page sought in the three Kings, Otis Rush, and Buddy Guy. In the process he invented a unique style of "team" guitar playing with Brian Jones, Mick Taylor, and, for over thirty years, Ron Wood. Based on the "telepathic" rhythmic interplay of Muddy and Jimmy Rogers in the classic Waters band of the early 1950s, it has been the spawning ground for countless blues-inflected riffs inspiring countless followers. As many people consider Keith Richards to be the heart of the Rolling Stones, their story is his story.

Keith Richards was an only child born on December 18, 1943 in Dartford, Kent, England to Herbert Williams Richards and the former Doris Maud Lydia Dupree. When he was less than a year old, with his father away in the army, he and his mum had to be evacuated from their home due to Nazi bombing during the waning years of WWII. Upon their return after the war they found it demolished and had to find a new residence. In 1948 Keith went to Westhill Infants School and enjoyed playing football (rugby) with his father as well as going on outings to the Isle of Wight. From the beginning he was apathetic about school, though he liked drawing and painting, along with history and English. Saturday morning movies really had his interest, however, and he loved American westerns the best. Roy Rogers was a particular favorite, and he wanted to be just like him and play the guitar. In 1951 he went to Wentworth Junior County Primary School where he met Mick Jagger for the first time. Jagger recalled that he liked Richard's interest in the guitar, but not Roy Rogers.

Richard's maternal grandfather Gus Dupree played guitar, fiddle, saxophone, and piano, and when young Keith went to visit him he was always drawn to the guitar. Finally, in 1958 for his fifteenth birthday, his mother bought him a cheap acoustic on the condition that he actually "play it," and his grandfather obliged by teaching him a few chords. By 1959 he was listening to Little Richard and playing hooky from school, with the poolroom his hangout of choice. A year later he was asked to leave school due to his truancy, but the headmaster took sympathy on the rebellious youth and enrolled him in Sidcup Art School to study advertising. At Sidcup he met Dick Taylor who played guitar with Jagger in an amateur R&B band. Unbeknownst to Jagger, the two started playing together in a country and western band, and Richards bought his first little amp to electrify his guitar.

In 1961 Jagger started attending the London School of Economics while Richards was still at Sidcup, and the two happened to meet by accident at the Dartford Railway Station one day and renewed their friendship. In what has become part of the lore of the Stones, the two talked about the Chuck Berry and imported R&B records that Jagger had with him and made plans to get together again to listen to each other's record collections. On the following occasion they realized that Dick Taylor was a mutual acquaintance, and the fateful decision was made for the three to join together in a band. Richards acquired a Hofner electric, and when Jagger heard Richards and Taylor play, he decided to move away from the guitar and concentrate on his singing and blues harp playing instead. Taylor switched to drums, Bob Beckwith shared guitar duties with Richards on a tiny 6-watt amp, and Allen Etherington shook the maracas. They played Chuck Berry and Jimmy Reed tunes and called themselves Little Boy Blue and the Blue Boys. Band members would come and go, but Richards and Jagger always remained as the core of the group.

In the spring of 1962 Jagger and his boys went to Ealing outside of London to see Cyril Davies and Alexis Korner's Blues Incorporated at the Ealing Blues Club (formerly the Ealing Jazz Club). Brian Jones, who had been playing guitar with Paul Pond (later Paul Jones, leader of Manfred Mann), had been sitting in regularly, and on this occasion they heard Brian Jones play "Dust My Broom." Jones, who had taken to calling himself "Elmo Lewis" in tribute to his idol, Elmore James, is credited with being one of the first to play electric slide guitar in England, and he certainly impressed Richards and Jagger. After the show Jagger spoke to Jones and informed him that he was planning to start a band. In the meantime, Jagger sent a tape of his band to Korner. He was promptly invited to join Blues Incorporated in the company of drummer Charlie Watts and bassist Jack Bruce for gigs in Ealing and at the Marquee Club in London. Concurrently he still practiced regularly with Richards and Taylor.

Jones put an ad in *Jazz News* looking for musicians to join his R&B band, and piano player Ian Stewart responded first. Geoff Bradford, a respected and excellent "pure" blues guitarist who was also into Elmore James, Muddy Waters, and John Lee Hooker (like Jones) was personally invited into the group. In the summer of 1962 Jagger attended one of Jones' rehearsals and then started bringing Richards and Taylor along for twice-weekly sessions. However, Bradford left when the band began playing Chuck Berry and Bo Diddley covers along with straight-ahead Chicago blues. Mick Avory (later of the Kinks) filled in on drums, and in July the band, now dubbed the Rollin' Stones by Jones, got their first big break when they subbed for Blues Incorporated at the Marquee Club, followed by engagements at the Ealing Blues Club. (Note: Dave Godin, a friend of Jagger's, told Bill Wyman that the name came from "Mannish Boy," where Muddy sings, "Ooh, I'm a rollin' stone," not from the single of the same name from 1950). It was Jones's band from the beginning, and he exercised his authority for years until his self-destructive and bizarre nature caused his rapid decline.

Meanwhile, Richards graduated from Sidcup Art School, and the Stones were in need of a permanent drummer as they scuffled. In the late summer of 1962 Jagger and Jones moved into a flat in Chelsea together and were joined shortly thereafter by Richards. Discouraged with their lack of gigs and progress, they decided to give it one more year to pan out, even as Jones tried to replace interim drummer Tony Chapman (late of the Cliftons, Bill Wyman's group) with Charlie Watts from Blues Incorporated. Drummer Carlo Little, who played with Screaming Lord Sutch, and bassist Ricky Fensen were often called upon for rhythm section duties, but mainly the Stones just rehearsed and listened to records—though an underground buzz about their sound was developing without their knowledge. In the fall the band played a gig without a drummer, and not long after Taylor left to finish his studies at the Royal College of Art. The split was amicable, and Taylor would go on to play in the Pretty Things and achieve a measure of success.

With the Stones needing a bass player (as well as a permanent drummer who satisfied them), Chapman, the good sport (!) approached Bill Wyman (real name Bill Perks), his old band mate from the Cliftons, about auditioning in December 1962. Apparently, the group was not impressed with Wyman's lack of blues experience, though they were keen on his substantially more professional equipment. In addition, he felt that they could not survive "playing 12-bar blues all night." After a few more rehearsals, however, he threw in with the group and played his first gig on December 14 at the Ricky Tick Club in Windsor.

1963 began as 1962 had ended, with the Stones still struggling for gigs and Richards, Jagger, and Jones literally starving in their Chelsea digs. Charlie Watts was approached again and basically told that he was in the band whether he liked it or not. Despite his major reservations about them making a go of it, he was coming around to R&B music, as opposed to the swing jazz that was his great love, and he went along with their request. On January 12 Jagger, Jones, Richards, Ian Stewart (piano), Wyman, and Watts played their inaugural gig together. (Note: The name went back and forth between "Rollin'" and "Rolling" for some time for apparently no rhyme or reason.) They continued to work regularly for the same low bread, but a type of snobbish blackballing occurred as the "jazz Mafia" of Chris Barber and Cyril Davies thought they were "too poppy" and "inauthentic," thereby costing them their gigs at the Marquee and the Flamingo. At the end of January, though, the band received a reply from the BBC concerning their application for an audition in April for the "Beeb's" *Jazz Club* show.

Two important contacts at this time were Giorgio Gomelsky, an influential promoter and club owner, and Glyn Johns, an engineer at IBC Studios who encouraged the Stones to record a demo tape. Gomelsky provided more and better-paying gigs, and Johns set up a recording date for March. They recorded Bo Diddley's "Road Runner" and "Diddley Daddy," "I Want to Be Loved" by Muddy Waters, and Jimmy Reed's "Honey What's Wrong" and "Bright Lights, Big City." Jones was proud of the results and especially happy that they were able to capture the Jimmy Reed sound so authentically, an unheard-of concept in England at that time. An IBC exec shopped the tape around to a half dozen labels, but it was uniformly turned down for not being commercial enough. The Stones were discouraged, but on the upside a real blues scene was developing around them with more bands and an audience receptive for the wild, sensual energy that emanated from the aggressive way the music was being interpreted. Their gigs increased in frequency as the crowds increased in number and enthusiasm. A steady engagement at Giorgio Gomelsky's Crawdaddy Club in Richmond got them a sizeable review in a local paper and would prove a major stepping stone. Another would be the acquisition of nineteen-year old Andrew Loog Oldham as the Stones' manager.

Oldham's limited experience was in pop PR, but he immediately got what the Stones were about with their sexual energy that made them both dangerous and alluring at the same time. A three-year contract was signed. The next thing Oldham did was insist that the burly Stewart stop performing live with the band—"six faces were too many for the fans to remember"—and become the road manager while only playing in the studio. On May 10 the Stones cut their first single, Chuck Berry's "Come On" b/w "I Want to Be Loved." Later in the month they found out that they had failed the audition of April 24 for the BBC show performed with Carlo Little and Ricky Brown subbing for Watts and Wyman, who still had day gigs. The BBC felt the singer sounded "too black," but were interested in having the band back touring US acts on the radio, an offer that was laughingly ignored. On May 14, however, Oldham met with Decca Records and released "Come On" quickly on June 7. Though the recording had also been rushed, and the Stones were so unhappy with it that they fought with Oldham over playing it live, it differentiated them from the pop Mersey Beat sound that was becoming the "mod" rage through the Beatles and other British acts.

The single only reached #26 in the U.K. but positive press was starting to build. In August the Stones made the first of twenty appearances on the influential and popular *Ready, Steady, Go!* TV show while breaking attendance records at the Crawdaddy Club and virtually everywhere else they appeared. Jones's somewhat erratic behavior and incredibly bad leadership (he had considered letting Jagger go at one point and also replacing Wyman and Watts) encouraged Oldham to consolidate his position of power. At the end of September the Stones were excited to be booked on a 30-date tour with the Everly Brothers, Bo Diddley, and Little Richard. Diddley was so impressed with *them* ("Brian was the only white cat that got my rhythm") that he wanted them to back him up on tour, which they respectfully declined. On October 7 they went back in the studio to record Lennon and McCartney's "I Wanna Be Your Man" b/w" Stoned," and it reached #12 on the U.K. charts. In an ironic payback for the generous "gift" of the composition, the Stones began outdrawing the Beatles at some venues. At the same time they took something else from the "Fab Four"—the revolutionary idea of taking a side trip from their cherished blues by starting to write original material.

1964 continued the growing madness, with screaming girls, a brutal round of sold out shows, and hyper press that either loved or hated them. The long hair was an issue as was the "bad boy" image cultivated brilliantly by Oldham. A sign of things to come was the recording of the first Jagger/Richards original composition, "Will You Be My Lover Tonight" b/w "It Should Be You." More significantly, however, was the recording in January of Buddy Holly's "Not Fade Away" b/w the original "Little by Little." It became their first U.S. single in May, and with "I Wanna Be Your Man" as the flip side it made a respectable showing at #48. In February the Stones recorded their first self-titled LP of mostly blues and R&B covers, and it reached #1 in the U.K (edging out the Beatles), remaining on the charts for fifty-one weeks. In May it was released in the U.S. where it hit #12. The same month they tried to meet their idol Chuck Berry when he toured the British Isles with Carl Perkins, but were inexplicably blown off. In June the first Jagger/Richards original song, "As Tears Go By" recorded by Marianne Faithful, was released and got into the U.K. Top Ten.

In June of 1964 the Stones made their first, epochal cross-country tour to the United States where they were met with a combination of hysteria, shock, and, in some cases, ignorant American behavior about their hair and dress. The highlight for the band had to be going to Chess Records in Chicago and recording what would be their second album. Bobby Womack's "It's All Over Now" (with the infamous line "half-assed games" that radio stations regularly censored) b/w the original "Good Times, Bad Times" was cut and released as a single, going to #1 in England and #26 in the U.S. A. Besides meeting Buddy Guy, Willie Dixon, and a friendlier (!) Chuck Berry the second time around, they got the thrill of their lives when Muddy Waters helped carry in their equipment for the session and later coolly referred to Jones by saying, "That guitar player ain't bad."

In August the Stones *Five by Five* EP was released and climbed to #1 in the U.K. Irma Thomas' "Time Is On My Side" b/w the original "Congratulations" rose to #6 in the U.S. after a September release and featured Keith's best Chicago blues guitar solo to date. *12 X 5* (an expanded *Five by Five*) was put out as an album in the U.S. only and showed the Stones' ever-growing popularity by going all the way to #3. In November they reached back to their ever-present blues roots with the Willie Dixon-penned Howlin' Wolf classic "Little Red Rooster" b/w the original "Off the Hook" and had it promptly strut to #1 in the U.K.On a tremendous roll, they also released their best original to date with "Heart of Stone" b/w "What a Shame" and watched it rise to #19 in the U.S.

The Rolling Stones No. 2, with a selection of still mostly R&B covers, began the pivotal year of 1965 by easily reaching #1 in the U.K..Their third American album, *The Rolling Stones, Now!*, with a mix of tunes from the previous U.K album along with other covers, scampered up the charts to #5 after a February release date. Later in the same month "The Last Time" b/w "Play with Fire" arrived containing Richards's and the Stones' catchiest riff to date, and it went #1 in the U.K. and #9 in the U.S. Though both tunes were credited to the up and coming songwriting team of Jagger/Richards, the A side was actually based on "This May Be the Last Time" by the Staple Singers from 1955. In May, however, the number one Richards/Stones (or possibly anyone else's) "riff" of all time was captured for posterity when "(I Can't Get No) Satisfaction" b/w "The Spider and the Fly" was put to tape in Chicago while the band was in North America on yet another riotous tour. The story of how Richards awoke in the middle of the night with the riff in his head and recorded it on a portable tape player before going back to sleep is another part of the band's lore. It naturally zoomed (the fuzztone guitar sound that Richards employed to such devastating effect was called a "zoom bass") to #1 in England but more importantly, it was the Stones' first #1 single in the U.S. A little over a year after their first American release, the Stones had conquered the "colonies" on the strength of their love and dedication to the blues by bringing America's only indigenous art form back home and flaunting it in the face (and ears) of an unwitting public.

Over 40 years after they began the Rolling Stones are still at it as performers with only three changes of personnel. *Beggars Banquet* from 1968, arguably their greatest album (or possibly anyone else's) was, unfortunately, the swan song for Brian Jones. Among many ironies, it is their bluesiest, root-siest recording but prompted him to bemoan the "fact" that the Stones had gotten too far from the blues for his tastes. In truth, his increasingly unpredictable behavior, fueled by outrageous alcohol and drug use, had led to a life of utter decadence, and his considerable musical talents had declined precipitously. He was at odds with the band in every way and was preventing them from touring in the U.S. due to a previous drug conviction. On June 8, 1969 it was bilaterally announced that he was leaving the band, to be replaced by twenty-year old Mick Taylor from John Mayall's Bluesbreakers. Three weeks later on July 2 he was found dead in his swimming pool at the age of twenty-seven. Meanwhile, Richards had his own drug demons to face down, and in the early 1970s they almost got him fired from the band by Jagger and put in jail by the British authorities. Fortunately for him and all concerned he beat the rap and has been mainly an abuser of alcohol and cigarettes only ever since.

Taylor was a brilliant lead blues guitarist, and his tenure in the band from *Let It Bleed* (1969) to *It's Only Rock 'n' Roll* (1974) took the Stones to an instrumental place that they had never been, even with Jones. In the process it freed Richards to really hone his patented rhythm style with the open G tuning that he learned, along with others, from Ry Cooder and Gram Parsons of the Byrds in 1968, and that takes hold from *Let it Bleed* on. In December of 1974, however, Taylor left the band on good terms for "personal reasons," to their dismay—particularly to that of Richards who was a true admirer of the younger man's musicianship. Ron Wood, late of the Faces with Rod Stewart, took his place, effectively becoming an interchangeable guitarist with Richards as they both played an intertwining rhythm/lead style that once again harkened back to the early Muddy Waters band and the early Rolling Stones. Richards had been hanging out with Woody for over a year and had played on his *I've Got My Own Album to Do* (as did Taylor), and they had also performed together as the New Barbarians. Now into the first years of the millenium "Woody" has been a Rolling Stone longer than Brian Jones and Mick Taylor combined.

In December 1985 the Stones longtime "invisible" piano player Ian Stewart died at the age of 47. A year later, due to a row with Jagger over the direction of the band (pop for Mick, rock for "Keef," of course) that resulted in a hiatus for the Stones, Richards went out on tour with the X-pensive Winos and released his first solo effort, *Talk is Cheap*, in 1988. It far outpaced Jagger's solo vanity recording *Primitive Cool* both critically and commercially, going gold in the process, and he followed it up with *Live at the Hollywood Palladium* in 1991. After the smashing success of the Stones' *Steel Wheels* tour in 1989, however, the "Glimmer Twins" reconciled and agreed to put the Stones' fortunes ahead of their solo projects, including Richards's second outing, *Main Offender* from 1992. In 1993 Bill Wyman "retired" from the band to pursue his interest in documenting the blues and performing and recording with his blues band the Rhythm Kings, and Darryl Jones became their touring bassist.

"The World's Greatest Rock 'n' roll Band" shows no sign of letting up as they commenced spectacular world tours in 1997, 1998, 1999, and 2002–2003. At sixty (!), the seemingly indestructible Keith Richards is as committed to the music and the life it entails as he ever was, rocking out and playing the blues with the energy and passion of a man *one third* his age.

The Blues Guitar Style of Keith Richards

Keith Richards has probably remained truer to his original blues and rock 'n' roll roots than any of his vaunted contemporaries and fellow countrymen. With the example of Chuck Berry and the early Muddy Waters band with second guitarist Jimmy Rogers as his lasting influences, he plays a primary palette of blues notes always in the service of the song—never to show off his chops (or lack thereof!). Keith has been pictured with many instruments over the years, but the Telecaster (including the cool, semi-hollow Thinline), Les Paul Custom, and Gibson ES-355 (like Chuck's) are his main squeezes.

Keith combines both his blues *and* rock 'n' roll tastes in the shuffle of Track 23. Locking his hand in the basic 6th-string root position of the E minor pentatonic scale at fret 12, he says his piece with phrasing and the dynamics that result, rather than by carefully selecting notes to run the changes. Like his mentor Chuck B, Keith is a fan of the harmony and double-string bend, and the ones in measure 1 are dandies. On beat 1 he bends the 6th (C#) up to the ♭7th (D) while sustaining the bluesy ♭3rd (G) on top, followed by E/B (root and 5th) to establish the I (E) chord tonality. He then rears up on C#/A (6th and 4th), creating D/B (♭7th and 5th) that is released and followed by B/G (5th and ♭3rd) and resolution to the root (E) on beat 4. Measures 3 and 4 (I) are variations on this theme, but measure 2 contains a startling dissonance with the root (E), 5th (B), and ♭3rd (G) played as an E minor triad triplet on beat 4. Thankfully he resolves this nasty business on beat 1 of measure 3 with the root! Over the IV chord (A) in measures 5 and 6 Keith turns the G/C# dyad of measure 1 into a smeary double-string bend that provides hair-raising tension. The Berry unison bend of the 5th (B) in measure 7 keeps the anticipation bopping along until it is resolved to the root in measure 8 (sparked by the liberal use of the ♭3rd, G). Showing his blues credentials in measure 9 over the V chord (B), Keith makes sure to point out the root (B) with a bend up from the ♭7th (A) followed by the same tone fretted on string 2. By the same token he makes B/G and C#/A in measures 10 (IV) function as the 9th/♭7th and 3rd/root to nail the tonality. On a "blues roll" now, he ambushes the E7 tonality in measure 11 with the root (E), ♭7th (D), "true blue note" of the ♭3rd (G) bent a quarter step, and then the root once again on beat 4. As there is no V chord, but instead a repeat of the I chord, Keith just keeps banging on the ♭7th and root, with a encore of the "true blue note."

Performance Tip: Bend the 6th up with your ring finger while holding the ♭3rd in place with your pinky in measure 1 and use the same two fingers for the same notes (both bent by pushing upwards) in measures 5 and 6. All of the other double-string bends in measures 1, 3, and 4 should be executed by pulling down with your ring finger. The exception is B/G on beat 1 of measure 4 that should be pulled *down* with your index finger.

Track 24 is one of the only non-12 bar progressions in the book and shows Keith's R&B side that he has so spectacularly succeeded in turning into a Midas touch for the Stones in tunes like "Gimme Shelter," "Brown Sugar," "Tumbling Dice," "Beast of Burden," "Start Me Up," and others. Dig that the eight-measure I (C)–IV (F) verse actually contains three chord changes—Cadd9 (I), F (IV), and C (I). The Cadd9 voicing in measures 1, 3, 5, and 7 is, quite simply, a second inversion (5th on bottom) C major triad (E/C/G) at fret 5 with the addition of the D note at fret 7 on string 3 as the 9th (or "add9" note). The F in measures 2, 4, 6, and 8 is a first inversion (3rd on bottom) major triad (F/C/A) in fifth position. E/C (3rd and root) suffices to imply C major in measures 6 and 8. (Note: Dig that the above-mentioned hits are all in open tunings. However, Keith is perfectly capable of playing his patented chord melody in standard tuning as shown).

Performance Tip: R&B accompaniment is all about phrasing, especially the syncopated variety shown. Pay particular attention to how the downbeat of beat 2 in every measure is accented, listening carefully to the audio track for assistance. For the Cadd9 chord, barre across fret 5 with your index finger and access the D note with your ring finger. If you maintain the same barre for the F chord, it will be a snap to add the root note with your middle finger and the A with your ring finger for the classic Keith Richards formation. It will then be easy to access the C dyad by removing your middle and ring fingers.

Keith Richards Selected Discography

England's Newest Hit Makers (Abko)

Beggars Banquet (Abko)

Let It Bleed (Abko)

Get Yer Ya Yas Out (Abko)

Sticky Fingers (Virgin)

Exile on Main Street (Virgin)

ROBBIE ROBERTSON
The Weight

Robbie Robertson has been a reluctant guitar hero compared to his peers. During his reign from 1968–1977 as leader of the Band, the critically acclaimed, quintessentially American roots rock group, he only soloed occasionally, preferring to write the bulk of their material while playing trenchant, bluesy fills and supportive rhythm guitar. When given the opportunity, however, as occurred during the filming of Martin Scorsese's documentary of their final performance, *The Last Waltz* in 1976, he demonstrated that he could blaze through the blues like a musical hit man.

Jamie Robbie Robertson was born on July 5, 1943 in Toronto, Canada to a Jewish father, who died a few years after his son's birth, and Rosemarie Myke Robertson, a Mohawk Indian born and raised on the Six Nations Reservation. The youngster spent his early summers on his mother's reservation with her relatives who exposed him to the blues and country music. Around the age of five or six he started taking guitar lessons from a cousin and was soon writing his first songs. Eventually his musical interests evolved from country to big band and the nascent rock 'n' roll that was developing in the early and mid-1950s. Like other aspiring guitarists of his generation, the instrument completely took over his life, and he dropped out of school at the age of fifteen to become a professional musician. In 1958–59 he gigged around Toronto with a number of bands including Robbie and the Robots, Little Caesar and the Consuls, and Thumper and the Trambones.

Photo © Jeffrey Mayer 1996/Star File

Robbie Robertson dressed to "Roll into Nazareth" and "put the load" on his Fender Telecaster with a fat humbucking pickup.

Concurrently, rockabilly and R&B guitarist Ronnie Hawkins (brother of Dale Hawkins of "Susie-Q" fame) from Arkansas was fronting his touring band Ronnie Hawkins and the Hawks with his homeboy, former guitarist turned drummer, Levon Helm. Garnering work in Ontario proved more rewarding financially than it did back in the American South, and he set up a base of operations around Toronto in 1959. When his regular piano player split in 1960 he approached a local cat named Scott Cushnie, who would only join if his bandmate Robertson could come along as well. As Hawkins already had a lead guitarist in Fred Carter, Jr., he reluctantly went along with the deal if Robertson would take over the bass from the departing Jimmy Evans. Ironically, Hawkins had recorded a composition called "Someone Like You" on his *Mr. Dynamo* album written by the then fifteen-year old Robertson in 1958. Carter would soon leave, opening up the lead guitar chair for Robertson as Rebel Paine assumed the bass chores. Guitarist

Rick Danko saw the Hawks perform and was so knocked out by their raw energy and excitement that he lobbied for a role and was brought in as another rhythm guitarist before switching to bass when Paine gave his notice. In 1961 Richard Manuel slid onto the piano bench in place of Cushnie. The final piece of the historical puzzle was Garth Hudson, a multi-talented musician with skills on keyboards and tenor saxophone who came on board the "band" wagon near the end of 1961. A classically trained pianist, he would only join if the other members paid him to give them lessons, a ploy developed to mollify his parents who were aghast at the thought of their son playing wild rock 'n' roll. For the obsessed Robertson it was nirvana as he got to solo night after night. Over time he would develop a devastating blues style with the rigid and demanding Hawkins that owed a debt to Roy Buchanan following the Tele master's short, mythical stint with the Hawks in 1961 (see *Roy Buchanan* entry).

In early 1964, after having recorded a number of singles with Hawkins, including an especially searing version of Bo Diddley's "Who Do You Love" b/w "Bo Diddley," the Hawks mutinied with Helm in tow. They added Bruce Bruno on vocals and Jerry Penfound on sax and lit out as the Levon Helm Sextet (soon changed to Levon and the Hawks) on hell-raising tours of the American South combined with regular work in Ontario. Penfound and Bruno left before too long, and in 1964 and 1965 the road-tested blues and R&B powerhouse recorded a few singles for the Ware and Atko labels in New York, under the name the Canadian Squires, in order to separate themselves from the Hawkins connection. The summer of 1965, however, would be a major turning point for the "band," a famous singer/songwriter, and the history of rock music. In the meantime, Robertson would be invited by acoustic country bluesman John Hammond, Jr. to play on his electric blues LP *So Many Roads*. And, in a tantalizing footnote of "what might have been," the Hawks would meet legendary blues singer and harpist Sonny Boy Williamson II for a jam. Just back from a tour of England where he was accompanied by the Yardbirds, among other British blues-rockers, he was looking for a group who really knew what he was about. Plans were made for the Hawks to back Williamson, but unfortunately he died before they could be put into place.

Without their knowledge, a Toronto secretary working for Albert Grossman, Bob Dylan's manager, recommended the Hawks as the group to back up the heroic folk singer on his initial electric tour of America, Europe, and Australia. During their swing through the eastern part of the U.S. Dylan traveled down to the Jersey shore from New York City to catch their blistering set before a revved up audience. He hired Robertson and Helm (at the former's insistence) to back him for gigs in New York and Hollywood with bassist Harvey Brooks and keyboardist Al Kooper following his landmark electric debut at the Newport Folk Festival, where he had been supported by the Butterfield Blues Band. Again at Robertson's insistence, the entire group was brought in behind Dylan after some rehearsal in Toronto during the early fall of 1965, and they all moved to New York. The constant booing from the folk "purists" at the Dylan gigs proved to be very upsetting to Helm, however, who was none too thrilled with the "bard's" music, either. He left and went south, despite Robertson's insistence that the music was still developing, and was replaced by Mickey Jones. Robertson was proved correct at a spectacular performance at the Royal Albert Hall in London in the spring of 1966—a brilliant, emotionally wrenching combination of rock, blues, and folk that defied easy classification.

Back in the U.S. Dylan moved from the Village to Woodstock, New York to work on the editing of a documentary film culled from the European dates. Before long the four "band" members had also moved upstate to West Saugerties in the Woodstock area. In the basement of a rented house dubbed "Big Pink" (due to its size and color) they got together daily with Dylan to rehearse and record songs in 1967 that would eventually come to be referred to as *The Basement Tapes*. The experience would be beneficial for all parties concerned, as Dylan would come to appreciate the value of "simpler" (especially lyrically) music like country and R&B. At the same time, the music played by Robertson, Danko, Manuel, and Hudson was evolving with Robertson's songwriting and overall artistic direction into a style of American popular music that evoked a pastoral, elegiac past that only ever existed in the imagination. Realizing the potential in the music swirling around his client, Albert Grossman became the group's manager and got them a contract with Capitol Records as Helm returned. At that point they became known simply known as "The Band" (short for the band that backed Dylan, though some misread it as *the* Band), and *Music from Big Pink* (that house!) was released in July 1968. It ran counter to the prevailing counterculture that reveled in revolutionary psychedelia and heavy blues rock as it contained thoughtful music made for listening rather than "boogying" (though it did rock, swing, and groove); the album and the group became the darling of the critics. It went to #30 and "The Weight," one of Robertson's most enigmatic tunes, made it to #63. *The Band* from 1969 was even better and more popular (#9) with the singles " Up on Cripple Creek," (#25) and "Rag, Mama, Rag" (#57). The epic "The Night They Drove Old Dixie Down," the most evocative and sympathetic rendering of the Civil War from the perspective of the South ever recorded, was included among the twelve selections that Robertson either wrote or co-wrote. He has since remarked how writing for Helm's remarkably expressive and quintessentially southern American voice (the only native-born U.S. citizen in the bunch) was a great inspiration. The Band appeared at the Woodstock Festival in August, but their recorded and filmed performance has never seen the light of day. In addition, they became the first North American rock group to be featured on the cover of Time Magazine.

The massive publicity, particularly as directed at the charismatic Robertson, began to change the dynamics within the Band, but not before they created another aural masterpiece with *Stage Fright* a year later. It charted even higher than their sophomore offering, hitting #5 with "Time to Kill" reaching a respectable #77 and containing a rare Robertson solo that smoldered. *Cahoots*, their fourth release in as many years, signaled the downward slide that seemed to be inevitable given the pressures and escalating drug use, though it still rose to #21 with "Don't Do It" (#34) and the ironic "Life is a Carnival" (#72), featuring memorable hot guitar licks, keeping their iconoclastic music on the airwaves. Starting to show signs of creative burnout, Robertson and the Band put out the live *Rock of Ages* in 1971 and a tepid collection in 1973 of the rock, blues, and R&B classics that they used to play in the Hawks called *Moondog Matinee* (#28). The single of Clarence "Frogman" Henry's "Ain't Got No Home" clocked in at #73, and their only significant public appearance that year was at the attendance-breaking Watkins Glen Festival at the racetrack in upstate New York with the Allman Brothers and the Grateful Dead. Reconnecting with their former mentor and sponsor, the Band backed Dylan on his *Planet Waves* and a major national tour in honor of their historic reunion. A live album with the legendary songster called *Before the Flood* was released in 1974 and became a huge, commercial success.

A year later they came back with renewed vigor on the all-new studio album *Northern Lights - Southern Cross* and were rewarded with a solid position at #26 on the charts. Helm and Hudson also played on the *Muddy Waters Woodstock Album* in a gesture that partly made up for their lost opportunity with Sonny Boy Williamson and did Waters and Chess Records a good turn at the same time. The release of a *Best of the Band* LP in 1976, before their final tour, seemed to confirm the ringing of the death knell as all the members were off and involved in their own professional and personal pursuits.

On Thanksgiving Day in 1976 the official end of the Band was commemorated by the filming of their final concert in San Francisco by movie director Martin Scorsese. Titled *The Last Waltz* with guest appearances by an all-star lineup of Muddy Waters, Dylan, Ronnie Hawkins, Eric Clapton, Neil Young, Van Morrison, Joni Mitchell, Neil Diamond (!), and others, it is a fitting, if self important, sendoff, with Robertson writing and singing lead on "Out of the Blues" for the occasion. Stepping squarely into the spotlight with his guitar for an epic duel with Clapton on Bobby "Blue" Bland's "Further on up the Road," he takes the full measure of Old Slowhand, while his position as the focal point of the group is shown throughout. His interview segments with Scorsese are particularly revealing, especially when he confides that Ronnie Hawkins promised him "more pussy than Frank Sinatra" when he joined the Hawks. The film and accompanying soundtrack was released in 1978, and the album gave a strong showing at #16. Meanwhile, in 1977 *Islands*, the Band's last studio album with Robertson, came out and notched at #64, but there was no supporting tour. Perhaps perversely, it contained his first lead vocal on "Knockin' John Lost."

Robertson and Helm tried pursuing acting careers in 1980 with *Carny* and *Coal Miners Daughter*, respectively, while Danko attempted to go solo with his music. Robertson was financially secure with the royalties from his numerous Band songwriting credits (openly questioned by Helm in his autobiography), but the other members up and decided they were not quite ready to call it quits after all. They reunited in 1983 with Earl Cate on guitar, but the death of Richard Manuel in 1986 made the several future reunions bittersweet affairs, all of which Robertson steadfastly boycotted. *Jericho* (1993), *High on the Hog* (1996), and *Jubilation* (1998, the Band's thirtieth anniversary) all contained the excellent lead guitar of Jim Weider, who by 1998 had actually been a member longer than Robertson. Rick Danko's death in 1999, however, seems to have pulled the final curtain on the Band as an ongoing ensemble, regardless of the personnel.

Robbie Robertson, in contrast, never looked back. Having established a relationship with Martin Scorsese, he would go on to score music for the director's *Raging Bull* (1980), *King of Comedy* (1983), and *The Color of Money* (1986). Intriguingly, it took until 1987, more than ten years after *The Last Waltz*, for Robertson to record his self-titled solo debut with guest spots from Hudson and Danko. It hit #38, went gold, and earned him a Grammy nomination for Best Rock Vocal. At the Juno Awards, Canada's version of the Grammys in 1989, Robertson received a slew of honors, and the Band was inducted into the Juno Hall of Fame while the group, minus Helm, reunited with Robertson for their first live performance together since 1976. In 1990 Robertson followed his debut with *Storyville* (#69), a concept album about the infamous red light district of New Orleans around the turn of the twentieth century. Recorded mostly in the Crescent City, it was nominated for Grammys for Best Rock Vocal Performance and Best Engineered Album. In 1994 the Band was inducted into the Rock and Roll Hall of Fame where they reunited to perform at the induction ceremony.

Since then Robertson has been exploring his maternal roots by recording *Music for the Native Americans* for a TV documentary series and *Contact from the Underworld of Redboy* (1998), both with the Native American group, the Red Road Ensemble. In 2000 he joined DreamWorks records as Creative Executive and composed the musical score for Oliver Stone's *Any Given Sunday*. At the XIX Olympics in Salt Lake City in 2002 he performed new versions of "Making a Noise" and "Stomp Dance (Unity)" from *Contact from the Underworld of Redboy*. The same year he served as music supervisor for Scorsese's *Gangs of New York*.

The Blues Guitar Style of Robbie Robertson

All those years of playing backup with Ronnie Hawkins, Bob Dylan, and, of course, The Band, trained Robbie Robertson to stay "in the pocket" and "in the harmony" by following the changes. Like anyone who has put in the time, he has enough chops to ignite his strings if needed, but rarely does. Teles and Strats (his custom color Strat in *The Last Waltz* has a humbucker substituted in the neck position) give him the necessary "bite" to make his succinct musical statements.

Robbie literally ranges the length of the fingerboard while sprinkling in a few "whistlers" in the slow blues of Track 25. In measures 1–4 (I) he relies on the open G string to define the tonality for the most part, with the blues-approved ♭3rd (B♭) adding some needed grit in measures 3 and 4. Maintaining continuity (but cleverly avoiding the root) in measures 5 and 6 over the IV chord (C), he still works the G string (5th) and fretted notes along with the major 3rd (E) briefly in measure 5 and the 9th (D) in both measures. Dig that playing G/D (5th and 9th) in measure 6 *could* be seen to imply C9 and that, in fact, Robbie bends the root (C) up to the 9th with smooth vibrato on beat 4. In measures 7 and 8 (I) he moves dynamically up the fingerboard to first the "B.B. King box" at fret 8 and then the next one up around fret 10, emphasizing the tonality-defining major 3rd (B). After resolving to the root (G) on beats 3 and 4 of measure 8, Robbie bends the 4th (C) up to the 5th (D) and sustains it across the bar line, where it becomes the root of the V chord (D) in measure 9, released down to the ♭7th (C). Relocating to the G blues scale at fret 15, he includes the fretted root and the 5th (A) bent up to the 6th (B). In measure 10 (IV) he combines the root (C), 9th (D), and ♭7th (B♭) notes for a solid C dominant tonality while resolving conclusively to the I chord with the 3rd (B), 5th (D), and root (G) in measure 11 for the turnaround. Unison bends to the 5th (G) suffice over the IV chord and then function as the root (G) on beats 1 and 2 of measure 12. On beat 4 Robbie moves to the V chord (D) with the ♭7th (C) bent to the root (D).

TRACK 25

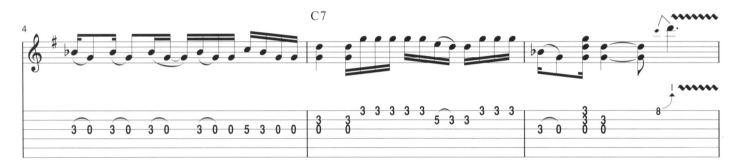

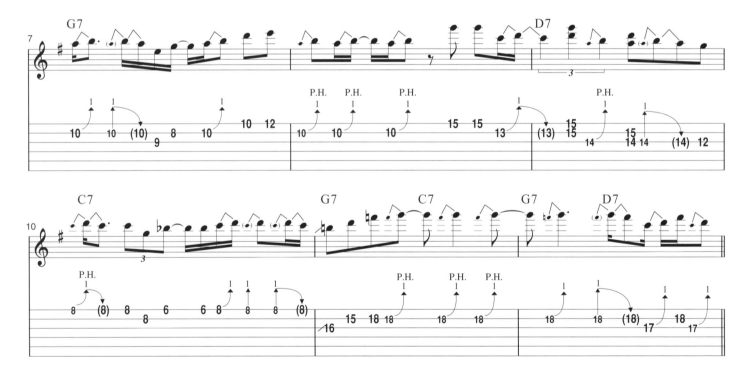

He hews even closer to the harmony of each change in the shuffle blues of Track 26. In measures 1 and 2 he uses the 4th (D) bent a half step to the bluesy ♭5th (E♭) while sustaining the ♭7th (G), followed by the root (A) in the basic blues box of the A minor pentatonic scale. The A/E (root and 5th) dyad in measure 3 also nails the tonality before Robbie makes his move to the blues box at fret 12 in measure 4 by bending the ♭3rd (C) up a quarter step to the "true blue note" followed by the 5th (E). A tasty run down the composite blues scale (blues scale plus Mixolydian mode) in measure 4 leaves the resolution hanging, thereby creating anticipation for the next measure by ending on the 5th (E) followed by a dynamic musical rest of a quarter note. Robbie jumps back down to the A minor pentatonic scale for measures 5 and 6, making sure to punctuate the root (D) along with the ♭7th (C), 5th (A), and 9th (E) for a rich and full dominant tonality. In measure 6 he continues to outline the D9 tonality with E/C (9th and ♭7th). Warming to the idea of double-stops, he swings G/E (♭7th and 5th) and A/E (root and

5th) dyads in measures 7 and 8 of the I chord. Showing off his skills as a trio-type guitarist capable of switching smoothly between lead and rhythm, he arpeggiates an E7 voicing in measure 9 for the V chord (E) and the top three notes of a D9 chord in measure 10 over the IV chord. He wraps it all up in the turnaround of measures 11 and 12 with runs down the A minor pentatonic and resolves to the root notes of the I (A) and V (E) chords, respectively. Observe the real deal blues bends to the "true blue note" on beats 1 and 4 of measure 11.

Performance Tip: In the pickup and measures 1 and 2, bend the 4th (D) up with your ring finger (backed by the middle and index fingers) while holding down the ♭7th (G) with your pinky. Play the G/E dyad in measures 7 and 8 with your ring and middle fingers, adding in the A note at fret 10 on string 2 with your pinky.

TRACK 26

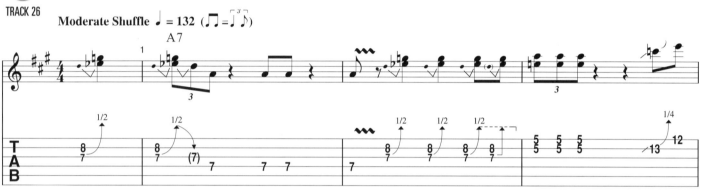

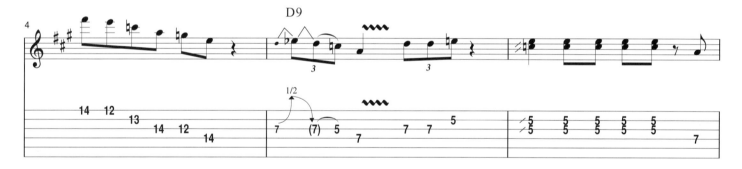

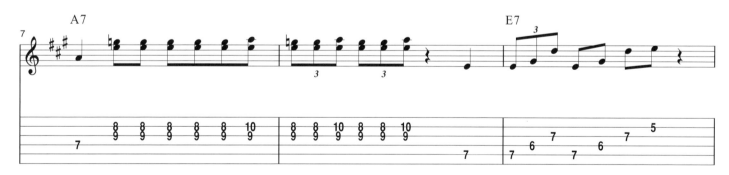

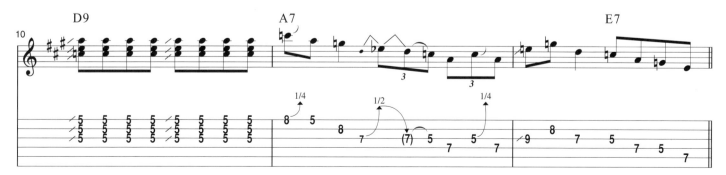

Robbie Robertson Selected Discography

With The Band:

Music from Big Pink (Capitol)

The Band (Capitol)

Stage Fright (Capitol)

Rock of Ages (Alliance)

The Last Waltz (Warner)

With Bob Dylan and The Band:

The Basement Tapes (Columbia)

MICK TAYLOR
Stone Alone

As Keith Richards said with accuracy, if not overstatement, "Mick Taylor was the only one to leave the Rolling Stones alive." Far more significantly, however, the deeply expressive lead guitarist brought a level of free-flowing blues improvisation to the pre-eminent British blues veterans that they have not experienced before or since. The fact that he had angelic and androgynous good looks to give Jagger a run for the attention of the young ladies did not hurt the appeal of the band, either. Showing extraordinary musical talent early on, the success that he achieved while still a very young man has made these accomplishments an extremely tough act to follow in his later years.

Photo by Robert Knight

Striking a pensive pose while showing off his strikingly good looks,
Mick Taylor coaxes celestial tones from his vintage Les Paul 'Burst.

Michael Kevin Taylor was born on January 17, 1949 to Lionel and Marilyn in Welwyn Garden City, England and grew up in Hatfield, a suburb of London. His mother played piano, and his father always encouraged his interest in music. Going with his parents to see Bill Haley and the Comets play at the Golders Green Hippodrome in 1955, in conjunction with hearing Elvis and the first generation of rock 'n' rollers, fired his musical imagination. In 1959 he attended Onslow Secondary Modern School in Hatfield. Around the age of eleven he was given some guitar lessons by an uncle, and within

a couple of years he was playing R&B and pop music with school friends. In 1963 he quit high school to work as a commercial artist and as a laborer in a paint factory. In his mid-teens in 1964–65 he played R&B and pop with local London bands the Juniors and the Gods (with guitarist Greg Lake and other band members who would go on to form Uriah Heep) before discovering the blues through the music of American rockers like Eddie Cochran and Chuck Berry. Buying a Chess Records compilation album exposed him to Muddy Waters and Little Walter. Seeing Muddy and Howlin' Wolf play in London while on British tours completely won him over, and he further advanced his blues education through the records of Buddy Guy, Freddie King, and later on, Albert King.

In 1966 he got his first big break by making it himself. At a John Mayall and the Bluesbreakers gig Eric Clapton failed to show, though his sunburst Les Paul and Marshall combo amp were sitting onstage. The seventeen-year old Taylor boldly went backstage and spoke to Mayall about filling in and was afforded the opportunity to play Slowhand's axe. Apparently he made a good impression on the audience and the boss, who took down his phone number after the gig. When Peter Green (Clapton's successor) left, Taylor got the call to come up to the blues big leagues in 1967. Though he still considered himself a beginner, he had enough confidence to accept the offer. He went straight out and purchased a 1958 Les Paul from Selmer's Music Shop in Charing Cross Road where another future Les Paul master, the late Paul Kossoff (Free, Back Street Crawler), was a salesman. Taylor ran the Paul through a 50-watt Marshall head with a 4 X 12 cabinet and eventually added an SG and a Strat to his arsenal. His first album with the royalty of the British blues scene was *Crusade* where he was prominently featured on Freddie King's instrumental "Driving Sideways," the Mayall/Taylor instrumental "Snowy Wood," and Otis Rush's classic "I Can't Quit You, Baby." As Greeny had smoothly slipped into Clapton's shoes, the young Taylor gave no reason for the band's fans to pine away for his predecessor, either. The connective tissue between the three modern blues masters, besides their common influences, was the fluid, sensuous vibrato that each possessed in spades.

Taylor was with the Bluesbreakers for two years until 1969, longer than any other guitarist, and also appeared on the experimental and jazzy *Bare Wires, Blues from Laurel Canyon,* and the live *Diary of a Band Vols. 1* and *2,* all in 1968. When Mayall informed him that he was making a change of direction, eschewing the heavy electric blues guitar of the past in favor of a stripped down acoustic sound for his album *Turning Point,* Taylor gave his notice. Mayall had known the Stones for years, and when they called him looking for a guitarist to fill in for Brian Jones, who had become a serious liability to the band at that point, the "Godfather of British Blues" knew what to do. He suggested Taylor, and the Stones invited him down to Olympic Studios for what he thought was going to be session work on their next album, *Let it Bleed.* The first tune he played on was "Live with Me," and the following day, to his shock and surprise, he was asked to join the band on a permanent basis as Jones would be given his walking papers. He was only twenty years old.

His time with the Stones, not including the landmark *Beggars Banquet* that started the ball (stone) rolling the previous year, would coincide with their period of greatest creativity. The acknowledged classics *Let it Bleed, Sticky Fingers* (1971), and *Exile on Main Street* (1972), not to mention the live *Get Yer Yas Yas Out* (1970), are rightly acknowledged as the best synthesis of blues-based rock ever recorded. Taylor's brilliance was encouraged and was given the opportunity to shine throughout, continuing on the lesser efforts of *Goat's Head Soup* (1973) and *It's Only Rock 'n' Roll* (1974) that followed. Unfortunately, his considerable (in his estimation) contribution to the writing of songs like "Can't You Hear Me Knockin'," "Sway," "Moonlight Mile," and "Time Waits for No One" eventually became a bone of contention between Jagger and Richards and Taylor, as he was never given any songwriting credits (except for "Ventilator Blues" on *Exile*). Combined with the epic decadence that took place on the numerous Rolling Stones world tours marked by his and Richard's use of heroin, Taylor opted out of the band in December of 1974. Richards would miss his musical camaraderie and wished him well, but Jagger was upset with Taylor and apparently carries a grudge yet.

In 1975 Taylor joined the Jack Bruce Band with keyboardist Carla Bley for a brief spell and a tour of Europe. He spent the next several years recording with Ron Wood, Mike Oldfield, and Little Feat, and finally released his long-anticipated, self-titled solo album in 1979. Despite the warm critical reception, the public did not embrace the pop rock sound with the killer blues-rock solos that seemed passé in the punk rock and new wave era. In 1981 he did a short tour and recorded with the Alvin Lee Band and in 1982 got back onstage with the Stones one night in Kansas City to the chagrin of Jagger, but the delight of the rest of the group. The same year he (and John McVie) reunited with John Mayall and his Bluesbreakers for a tour, maintaining a good relationship with his former mentor that lasts to the present. In 1983, while still touring with Mayall, he played with Mark Knopfler on Bob Dylan's *Infidels* album (he had previously appeared on *Dylan* in 1973), leading to a productive relationship with the rock poet that lasted into 1984 with another tour and a couple of live recordings.

Taylor moved to the U.S. in 1986, living in New York City for a while where Richards joined him onstage at the old Lone Star Café for a jam. During the next few years he played small gigs with various band members up and down the East Coast and in 1989 was inducted into the Rock and Roll Hall of Fame with his old mates. In 1990 he toured with Carla Olson, the roots rocking Textones' guitarist and singer who encouraged him to perform his best recorded material like "Sway." The same year he released his second solo album, the great, live blues extravaganza *Stranger in This Town* followed by the live *Too Hot for Snakes* (with Olson) in 1991. Taylor relocated to Los Angeles that same year and played on John

Mayall's *Wake Up Call,* as well as Olson's *Within an Ace* (1993) and *Reap the Whirlwind* (1994) before moving back to England in 1994, from whence he initiated yet another tour of Europe. In 1995 he issued the uneven *Live at the 14 Below* with American tenor sax vet Joe Houston and generally kept busy picking the strings.

His third solo album in a little over twenty years (!), *A Stone's Throw,* was released in 2000, and despite the obvious (some would say shameless) reference to his illustrious past, it is a fine, mature production. His records have expanded to include jazz, Latin, pop, and rock music, as well as the ever present blues that is his heritage and lifeblood. His standard-tuned slide playing, in particular, while always strong and distinctive, has evolved into a singular voice worthy of comparison with one of his heroes, Earl Hooker. In 2001 Carla Olson recorded *Ring of Truth,* her first album in six years, and she remembered to "ring" up her old pal Mick for accompaniment and to be featured on several extended guitar showcases. A guest spot on the John Lee Hooker tribute album *From Clarksdale to Heaven* and with veteran blues keyboardist Barry Goldberg on, appropriately enough, *Stoned Again* (a Stones tribute album produced by Olson), along with the perennial tour of Europe, occupied his time in 2002.

The Blues Guitar Style of Mick Taylor

Much has been made of how the Stones took their music to a whole new level in the years 1968–74 based to a large extent on the sensuous blues soloing of Mick Taylor. Though he adapted his style to blend in and complement that of the band, he was in fact just continuing to play with the same smokey intensity begun with John Mayall and the Bluesbreakers. Like his fellow former 'Breakers Clapton and Green, he managed to tap into another reality, far removed from the British Isles, at an early age. The vintage sunburst Les Paul was his trademark axe for many years, but the Strat (what a surprise!) has also become a favored instrument.

Track 27 is a slow blues filled with the dramatic dynamics and the distinct linear playing (related to his slide work?) for which he is justly lauded. Right off notice how the root note of the I (E) and V (B) chords, along with the 9th (B) of the IV (A), are sustained in measures 1, 5, and 9, respectively. In measures 2 and 3 Mick employs the basic and extension positions of the E blues scale (including the hip ♭5th, B♭) above fret 12 to create tension that is resolved to the root (E). The C♯ relative minor pentatonic scale at fret 9 is used in measure 4 with emphasis on the ♭7th (D), 5th (B), 4th (A), and finished off with the G♯/E (3rd and root) dyad. Over the IV chord (A) in measure 6, following the sustained bend of the 9th, Mick releases the bend down to the ♭7th (G) and treats us to blues heaven for two beats.

Measures 7 and 8 (I) contain snakey lines from the E composite blues scale (blues scale plus Mixolydian mode) all played on the G string with the well-chosen notes of the 4th (A), ♭3rd (G), 9th (F♯), and ♭7th (D) ending with sustained and vibratoed resolution to the root (E). Following the sustained root (B) of the V chord in measure 9, Mick locks into the E blues scale at fret 12 for the 5th (E), 4th (D), 9th (B), and root (A) notes over the IV chord. He slinks through the turnaround in measure 11 on string 1 with the root (E), 9th (F♯), and ♭3rd (G) of the I (E) chord and the ♭7th (G), root (A), 6th (F♯), and 4th (D) of the IV (A) chord. In measure 12 he bends, sustains, and vibratoes the root (E) of the I chord before resolving down the scale to the root (B) of the V chord on beat 4.

Performance Tip: In measure 2 anchor your index finger at fret 14 for beats 1 and 2 and use either your ring or ring and middle fingers to access the other notes. On beats 3 and 4 shift your index finger down to fret 12 and play the A note at fret 14 with your ring finger. Use a similar approach in measure 3. In measures 4, 7, and 8 you *could* play all the notes and glisses with your index finger. Play the E, F♯, and G notes in measure 11 with your index and ring fingers, sliding your ring from the F♯ to the G. Continue by sliding with your ring from the G to A notes that follow and end up by playing the G, F♯, and D notes with your ring, middle, and ring fingers. Listen to the audio to catch the phrasing of those groovy quarter-note triplets!

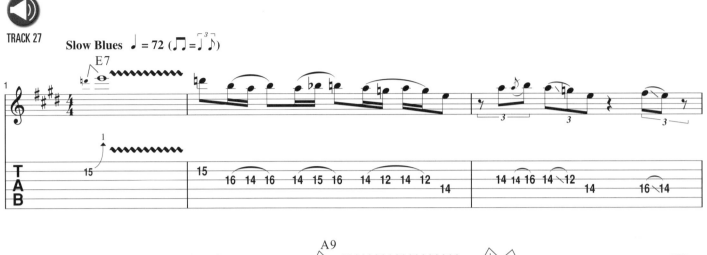

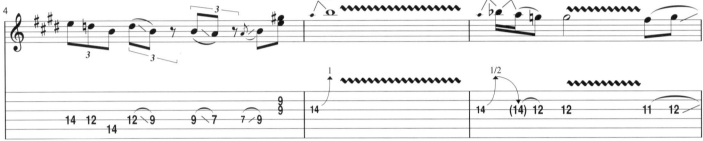

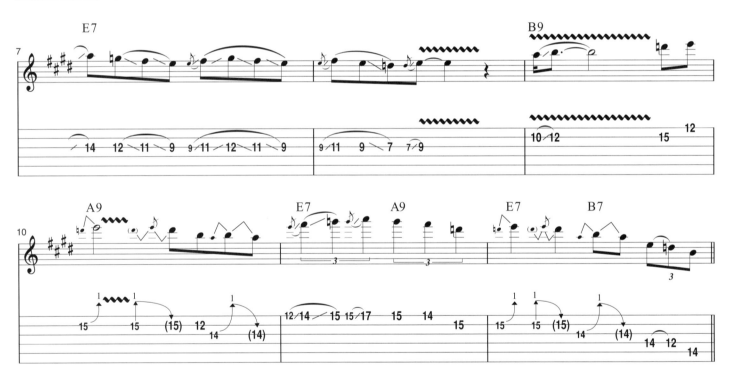

The slide-meister is displayed in all his melodic glory in Track 28. With the A blues scale in four "boxes" as his improvisational territory to be explored, Mick glides over one memorable line after another. Be sure to catch the repetition of notes throughout as a motif. In measures 1–4 he climbs up the fingerboard from fret 10 to fret 17, spotlighting the root (A) and 5th (E) in measures 1, 3, and 4 and the root (D), ♭7th (C), and 5th (A) in measure 2 for the IV chord (D). Dig the honking bass string runs on beats 2, 3, and 4 that emphasize the ♭7th (G), 6th (F♯), and 5th (E). For his turnaround in measures 11 and 12 Mick plays it pretty straight with the root notes over the I, IV, I, and V chords.

Performance Tip: Because Mick plays so linearly it is not as critical to be constantly muting. Nonetheless, in order to avoid picking up unwanted frequencies, it is imperative to lightly drag your ring, middle, and index fingers behind the slide (worn on the pinky, of course!) and drop the heel of your right hand down on the strings in front of the bridge in between notes for a more articulated sound.

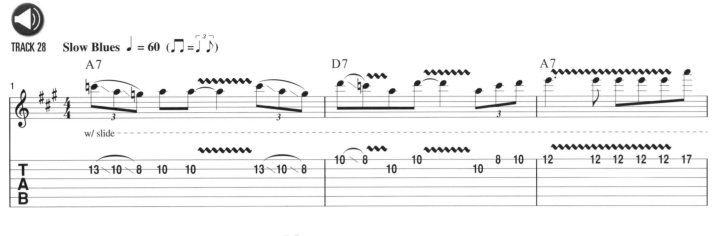

Mick Taylor Selected Discography

With John Mayall and the Bluesbreakers:
Crusade (Mobile)

With the Rolling Stones:
Let It Bleed (Abko)
Get Yer Ya Yas Out (Abko)
Sticky Fingers (Virgin)
Exile on Main Street (Virgin)

Solo:
Mick Taylor (Columbia)
Stranger in this Town (Maze/Kraze)
Too Hot for Snakes (Razor & Tie)
A Stone's Throw (United States)

MICK TAYLOR INTERVIEW

How did you feel following Peter Green and Eric Clapton in the Bluesbreakers, and how did John Mayall handle it with you?

He didn't have any problem with it at all and took it well in his stride. He'd had three different guitar players by the time I arrived on the scene. He seemed to have a lot of faith in me and no doubts whatsoever that I would fit in. I was more nervous about joining him and following in the footsteps of Eric Clapton and Peter Green than I was when I joined the Rolling Stones. I was only seventeen years old, and it was much more of a musical challenge. I think I was one of his longest-serving guitar players until recent times.

John was a really good bandleader and always had a sense of what direction he wanted to go in. He liked to change things and change the lineup of the band, and he had a different concept for each album that we did. He never told anyone what to play and encouraged me to start writing—"No Reply" and some instrumentals. He's a legendary blues figure and should be in the Rock and Roll Hall of Fame, and I even wrote them a letter and told them so.

After you left the Stones your music changed from straight, traditional blues and R&B.

Not changed, but broadened. I've never really been a blues purist. I feel that every good blues guitar player, for instance, Eric Clapton, Jeff Beck, myself, Peter Green—we all had our own style, sound and way of interpreting blues. I always listened to jazz *and* blues. My first solo album in 1979 had a collection of vocal songs and instrumentals that are quite varied, but are hopefully held together by my guitar playing that is firmly rooted in the blues.

I have a whole collection of recordings that have not been released that I suppose people would call "jazz-blues fusion," though I don't like to put labels on what I do. In 1990 I recorded some music in New York with Max Middleton [jazz keyboardist - Ed.] that is mostly instrumental and really good. It's probably some of the best playing I've ever done.

How do you feel now about your playing with the Stones?

I'm obviously better known for what I did with the Rolling Stones than anything else, because it was the biggest, most commercial, most popular thing. But, I think my guitar playing is a lot more interesting and better now than it was then. However, people are not really aware of it because it's not on huge-selling albums like *Exile on Main Street* or *Sticky Fingers* that they know and love.

Who were some of your influences?

The same guys who influenced a whole generation of English musicians in the early 1960s: Buddy Guy, Junior Wells, B.B. King, Freddie King, and Jimi Hendrix, whose influence is still phenomenal, really. Their music and that of others is so much more accessible now in terms of what's available on CD and in the archives than it was when I was growing up in England in the late fifties, early sixties. You really had to seek this kind of music out, because it was only available in a few specialty record shops. I'm part of that early British blues scene that started with John Mayall and the Rolling Stones and various other people. For some reason we were all turned on by American R&B music.

It's a phenomenon that you and others were listening to that music at a time when most white Americans were not.

It's a sociological one, isn't it, that's related to racial segregation. In the sixties, if you wanted to hear black music you had to go to a black club in the ghetto. What people now refer to as the "British Invasion" was just American music recycled for white, middle class Americans, if you like. It made it more accessible and exciting, and in a way it's what kind of popularized blues music over the years. I know from experience that when I used to come over to America in the sixties I used to go to the South

Side of Chicago, Harlem in New York, or Watts in Los Angeles to buy old Elmore James or Muddy Waters records. You couldn't just go into any record store and buy that kind of music. And, it was pretty much the same in England. The only difference was that James Brown, Ike and Tina Turner, and even the Chicago blues guys used to come to Europe and tour, and I think that's why we all heard that music.

What other music do you like outside the blues genre?

I like flamenco music, but that's something I would listen to at home and maybe try and play on acoustic guitar. I actually did a show in Spain once with a Spanish blues band that was basically an evening of music with Spanish musicians and I was fortunate to meet this young, Gypsy flamenco guitar player. First he played on his own and then with us, and it was an interesting combination of styles.

I also like Latin American music and always have. Some of the stuff we play on stage, especially when we use a percussionist, is a little bit Latin-influenced—what you might call being like Carlos Santana. We have an instrumental called "Going South" that was recorded on *Stranger in This Town,* a live album from 1990.

What kind of music do you play with your current band?

I'm very much an electric guitar player when I'm with my own band, and the music is R&B with jazzy influences, rather than straight ahead rock 'n' roll.

It's great to hear you play so much slide guitar.

Yeah, I play lots of slide guitar now and I play in standard tuning, which is quite unusual.

Strictly in standard tuning?

No. If we're doing something traditional, I'll use a traditional Delta blues tuning like open E, open A, or open G, which is the tuning for "Honky Tonk Woman." But, I have found over the years that I can play regular guitar and slide at the same time. It's like having the little finger on my left hand be a "glass finger." I can use three fingers to play notes or a phrase or a run and then use the slide to play the next note up, where other guitarists would be fingering it with their little finger. It's an interesting way of playing. There are not too many people who do it, but there is one very, very good blues guitar player from the old school, who used to play with Muddy Waters, named Earl Hooker, who played like that. When I heard that really bittersweet sound he gets I was very impressed by it, and that's when I started playing the same way.

Do you always uses a glass slide?

Yes, a light glass slide, because a brass slide would be too heavy and you would have to have your guitar set up specifically for slide, which would then disable you from playing in a regular style. I have to adjust my action so it's somewhere in between. When I first started playing this way it was very hard to bend the strings and quite physically demanding, but I've gotten used to it.

Do you use a pick or the bare fingers on your right hand?

Fingers for everything, not just slide.

Have you ever done any formal study on the guitar?

No, just a lot of practicing. I play the piano quite a bit at home and I tend to write on the piano and then transpose to the guitar. I also play solo acoustic guitar at home and I like to experiment with different tunings like open E, but without using the slide. You can get different inversions of chords that way.

Do you read music?

Very poorly. I have a very good ear and understanding of harmony, though it's just instinctive, really. I don't think it's something that can be taught. You can teach people how to read music, but you can't teach them how to play.

Are there any new areas of guitar music you would still like to explore?

Well, I don't like to use the word new because I don't think there's anything new under the sun. Music is something that's always been there and every guitar player, or any good musician, just seems to absorb different influences and then express them in their own way. When I think about it, the only R&B guitar player who not only influenced other blues guitar players, but every guitar player, and changed the way people approach the guitar, is Jimi Hendrix.

That's not so apparent in your playing.

Not on records so much, but in the live shows it is. It's there all the time, but we just play differently on stage, like every band, especially with our kind of music. We tend to use the same approach as jazz musicians on some songs. The Hendrix influence would come out the most when we are playing blues.

You were with Mayall and the Bluesbreakers on the famous show with Albert King and Hendrix in San Francisco in 1967 that was recorded and became Live Wire/Blues Power.

Yes, Albert King was wonderful, Jimi Hendrix was wonderful, and I guess we were pretty wonderful, too. That was the first time I met Hendrix and I got to play with him, too. I also got to jam with him back in the West End of London at a club called the Speakeasy when he sat it with the Bluesbreakers.

Would he play straight-ahead blues when he sat in?

Yes, but nothing was that straight-ahead with him because he was such a phenomenal guitar player. It was because of those opportunities to see him and play with him so many times that I realized what a wonderful blues player he was, since he didn't just stick to straight blues on his albums.

Was it an intimidating experience to play with him?

He was a very shy, soft-spoken person, but onstage he was explosive. I think that every guitar player who was around at the time was pretty much in awe of him. Certainly Eric Clapton, Pete Townshend, myself, Jeff Beck, and everybody who had a name and were well known at the time found it impossible to not be influenced by him.

You all had your own individual styles, however, even at that point.

Yeah, I suppose you're right. Me and Eric Clapton and Peter Green had more of a traditional blues feel, and Jeff Beck had his own sort of style, as well. But, it was pretty much American music that we were all playing when we started.

LESLIE WEST
Mountain Man

Leslie West may be the most famous blues-rock guitarist to hail from the rugged shores of Long Island, New York. Along with his size and atypical background, almost everything about the big man runs counter to the prevailing notion of a guitar hero. That said, during his heyday of the 1970s West played some of the toughest (some would say the loudest, too), most incisive licks around. Adding to his distinction, he possessed an amazingly expressive vibrato and a fat, honking signature tone greatly admired by his fans and peers.

Leslie Weinstein was born on October 22, 1945 in an Army hospital in Forest Hills, New York. His father's rug cleaning company provided the amenities for a comfortable upper middle class existence, but when his parents separated he went to live with his mother. An uncle, Will Glickman, was a writer for the Jackie Gleason Show, a fact that would figure heavily into the launching of West's career to becoming a famous rock guitar player. Invited to a taping of the show in 1956, eleven-year old West arrived at the studio with his grandmother only to find that it had been cancelled. In its place they were allowed in to see Tommy and Jimmy Dorsey's *Stage Show* with Elvis as one of the guests. West would later state that the experience of seeing Scotty Moore with the King "Changed my life," and not long after, his grandfather bought him a used tenor guitar in a pawnshop. West eventually learned the requisite three (I, IV, and V) chords and performed "Heartbreak Hotel" in a seventh grade talent show at Halsey Junior High School two years later.

Photo © Jim Cummins 1998/Star File

A mountain of a man hollering for his "Mississippi Queen," Leslie West pointedly plucks his Gibson Flying V.

Coming from a broken home, along with his total boredom in class, likely contributed to his attending more than ten private schools. After finally quitting in the tenth grade in 1961 he went to work as a jeweler in the diamond district on West 47th Street in Manhattan. Coincidentally, "music row" was a block away on West 48th Street, and he began hanging out at the famous Manny's Music until one day he failed to return to work. He had received a Strat for his Bar Mitzvah in 1958 but was still smitten by the guitars hanging tantalizingly in the music store windows. He traded the beat up old (vintage) Fender for a shiny new Kent (!), to his later regret. Around fifteen or sixteen he started to practice a little more, learning chords from Bob "Waddy" Wachtel, who lived in West's building at the time and went on to have a career as a noted session cat in the seventies and eighties. At this point West formed a very loosely organized band called the Vagrants with his brother Larry and a few other friends.

The final push to get his act together came in 1964 when he saw the Beatles at Forest Hills Tennis Stadium. After that the Vagrants decided to get serious, playing Beatles tunes and soul and R&B covers like "In the Midnight Hour" and "Respect," with a few originals thrown in. A footnote to rock history is that the Vagrants recorded a version of the Otis Redding-penned soul classic "Respect" before Aretha Franklin. Unfortunately, it got ignored in favor of the flipside due to the Vagrants' manager owning a piece of the publishing.

Besides playing out on Long Island, with bands like Billy Joel's Hassels opening for them, the group cut a number of singles for Vanguard between 1965–68. While they were ensconced in a steady gig at the Rolling Stone Club on Second Avenue in 1965 they met the Rascals. The white soul group, mining similar territory based around the sound of the organ instead of the guitar, graciously introduced them to an agent who helped them record a demo and then negotiated a deal with Atlantic Records. Besides engineer Tom Dowd, who worked on "Respect" and would go on to fame with Cream, Clapton, and others, they met producer/guitarist/bassist Felix Pappalardi who was sent by Atlantic to record the band. After the single was in the can the Vagrants broke up, but Pappalardi told West to stay in touch as he went off to England to produce *Disraeli Gears* for Cream.

Coincidentally, West had caught Cream at the Fillmore East in 1968 and was completely enthralled with Clapton's playing, adding Slowhand's influence to that of Albert King, Keith Richards, and Jimi Hendrix. As soon as Pappalardi returned in 1968 West called him up to come down and hear his new group. Pappalardi dug what he heard but wanted the drummer replaced, as well as the bassist, whose position he ended up taking himself almost by default. Along with Norman D. Smart on drums and Steve Knight on keyboards, Pappalardi and West went into the studio in early 1969 to record *Leslie West - Mountain* which hit a respectable #72 on the charts, and West talked Pappalardi into going out on the road with the band. From there things started moving quickly as the group, also known as *Leslie West - Mountain*, made an excellent debut at the Fillmore West in San Francisco in July followed by dates at the Whiskey-A-Go-Go and Winterland. Coming directly on the heels of the breakup of the much beloved Cream, they were poised to fill the heavy blues-rock void and had a built-in audience ready for the transition. Their fourth gig and first on the East Coast was, amazingly, at Woodstock in August, arranged because they had the same agent as Jimi Hendrix. After the landmark festival the band would henceforth be called Mountain.

Before their official debut *Climbing!* was released in the summer of 1970, at West's behest N.D. Smart was replaced by Corky Laing, who had been functioning as his unofficial roadie. Originally from Montreal, he and West had known each other since the mid-1960s when they were both gigging in the New York City area, and they would go on to have a long personal and professional relationship that continues today. Driven by West's full-bore guitar attack and his gruff vocals, the album was a hard rocking smash, selling over a million copies and buoyed by the classic riff rocker, "Mississippi Queen" (#21). Pappalardi showed West how to get Clapton's saxy tone from *Disraeli Gears* with his Les Paul Junior (similar to Clapton's Gibson Les Paul Special, as they both featured the bite of vintage P-90 pickups) ramped up through a Marshall amp. One of its other outstanding tracks, the classically influenced "Theme from an Imaginary Western" written by Jack Bruce (originally for Clapton), would prove to be a preview of things to come.

Nantucket Sleighride (referring to a harpooned whale pulling a whaleboat in its wake), Mountain's second release in early 1971, sailed to #16, while the single "The Animal Trainer and the Toad" showed up at #76. Before the year was out Mountain would also release *Flowers of Evil*, but the breathless pace of their ascent up the rock ladder of success was already taking its toll. Despite a decent showing at #35, the material was thin in direct contrast to West's substantial girth, with only four new tunes and the second side of the LP filled up with a twenty-five-minute rock 'n' roll medley called "Dream Sequence" and a live version of "Mississippi Queen." A live album, *Mountain Live (Road Goes on Forever)* in 1972 contained an epic version of "Nantucket Sleighride" that took up the entire second side of the album, but instead of the death of a whale (no pun intended), it signaled the end of the original incarnation of Mountain. Pappalardi wanted to return to producing, citing hearing damage due to the excessive volume of Mountain in performance. (Note: The author saw the band around this time, and no one was louder than Pappalardi himself). While Pappalardi was away in England, West fired Steve Knight (whom he always disliked) and with his drummer friend in tow, joined with Jack Bruce to form West, Bruce, and Laing (Pappalardi was retained as part manager and part publisher). The obvious comparison to Cream was even more ironic, as Pappalardi had always been against going out as a trio for just that reason. Though it may have reflected his antipathy to Clapton at the time more than his actual musical opinion, Bruce commented that West was the best guitarist he had ever played with. WB & L recorded *Why Dontcha* (1972) and *Whatever Turns You On* (1973) before Bruce split in mid-1973, and their third LP (the charm?) *Live and Kickin'* was released in 1974.

West and Laing stayed together as Leslie West's Wild West Show. However, before long, West, Pappalardi, and keyboardist Bob Mann, with drummer Alan Schwartzberg filling in for the sick Laing, reformed as a new Mountain for the live double album, *Twin Peaks*, recorded in Osaka, Japan in mid-1973. From there on until the late 1980s the bass chair was connected to a revolving door. A year later *Avalanche* came out with Pappalardi and Laing minus Knight, but with rhythm guitarist David Perry instead. By 1975 Mountain was kaput again, and West commenced the Leslie West Band. *The Great Fatsby* was released with Don Kretmar (from the Blues project) on bass and Mick Jagger on guitar (!) for "High Roller," a "Brown Sugar" knockoff credited to Jagger, Richards, West, and Laing. The Leslie West Band followed in 1976 with guitarist Mick Jones, later of Foreigner fame, and Kretmar and Bill Gelber handling the bass chores. By now West was covering a much greater variety of original and cover material that allowed his guitar prowess to expand beyond blues-rock riffing into more melodic territory. Alas, drug abuse finally caught up with him, and he dropped out of the scene for a while, giving private guitar lessons in Manhattan. Adding to his personal woes, in 1983 Felix Pappalardi was shot dead in New York by his wife Gail Collins in response to the bassist's affair with a younger woman.

In 1985 West reformed Mountain again with Laing and British bassist Mark Clarke (Coliseum) to record *Go for Your Life*. Following the inevitable split, West brought Jack Bruce back "one more time!" for *Theme* in 1988. The same year he played on the all-instrumental, all-star *Guitar Speaks* ("Let Me Out A' Here") and the live *Night of the Guitars* ("Theme for an Imaginary Western") for Illegal Records, a subsidiary of I.R.S. Records. Performing as a solo act now, West released *Alligator* in 1989 with fusion bassist Stanley Clarke and drummer Steve Loungo and other session musicians. Four years later he returned with *Leslie West Live* and *Dodgin' the Dirt* with drummer Kevin Neal and bassist Randy Coven, also augmented by studio musicians. In 1994, Laing was back with West and ex-Jimi Hendrix bassist Noel Redding for a reconstituted Mountain, and the next year they recorded two tunes for the Mountain compilation *Over the Top*. *As Phat as It Gets* in 1999 was West's last solo album, and it found the considerably slimmed-down guitar hero playing leaner and meaner, too. In recent years he has once again performed as Mountain with Laing and bassist Richie Scarlet, as loud and proud as ever.

The Blues Guitar Style of Leslie West

Despite his outlandish behavior in the past, Leslie West is no flash guitarist. Instead, he goes for the right notes with a big, *phat* tone embellished with as expressive a vibrato as any bonafide blues legend. He made his bones with cool, vintage Les Paul Juniors but has played Steinbergers in later years. He helped design Westberger and Edberger guitars that he endorses and currently plays.

Leslie cuts right to the heart of the matter with a minimal number of hip "blues notes" and plenty of musical space in the fast boogie of Track 29. Using the basic E blues box in measures 1–3 and the E major pentatonic scale in measure 4, he resolves to the root (E) in measure 2 (and 3 and 4) after creating tension in measure 1 with the 4th (A) bent to the 5th (B). Dig how he ends the measure on the 5th (E) in anticipation of measure 7 (I) where he just plays the ♭7th (D) bent to the root (E). Seesawing back and forth between tension and release, Leslie emphasizes the grubby ♭3rd (G) and 4th (A) in measure 8 over the I chord before bending from the 5th (F♯) to the sweet 6th (G♯) in measure 9 over the V (B). In measure 10 (IV) he makes an unusual move to the E composite blues scale (blues scale plus

Mixolydian mode) that yields the 9th (B), 3rd (C♯), 5th (E), and ♭7th (G) notes for a superb dominant tonality. Defying convention even further he does not resolve to the root in measure 11 of the I chord, but rests and then bends the 5th (B) up to the melodic 6th (C♯). Not giving in at all, he continues bending to the 6th in measure 12, ending on a literal "high note."

Performance Tip: Developing a "singing" vibrato takes years and great attention to the subtleties of pitch and speed. Mike Bloomfield once said that one of the secrets to sustaining bent notes was "steady pressure," and the same could be said for achieving the best vibrato.

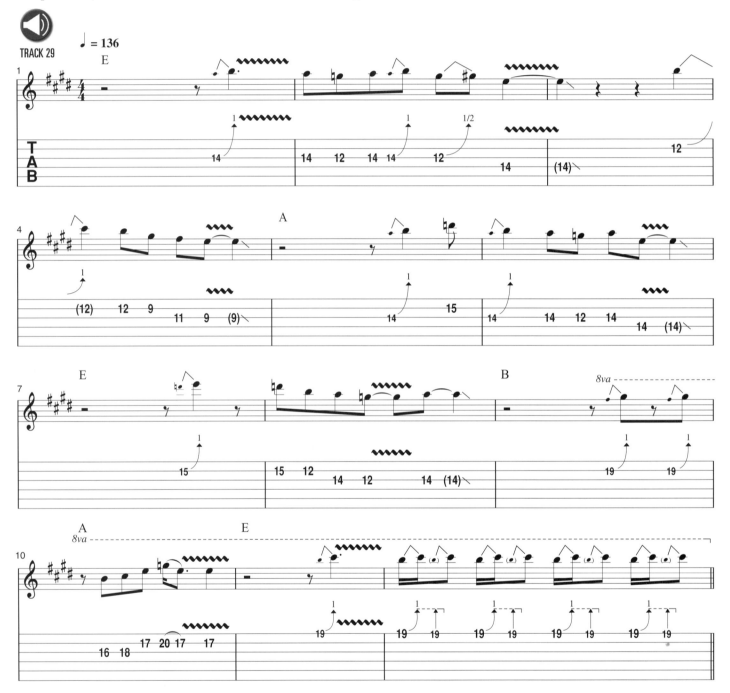

Track 30 contains a slow blues with fluid bends and vibrato featured in almost every measure. Leslie starts off atypically in the open position of the E blues scale with some old fashioned "country blues" licks and the low, open E string providing the I chord (E) tonality. In measure 2 over the IV chord (A) and measures 3 and 4 (I) he ambles up to the "B.B. King box" of the E scale, popping the root notes in measures 2 and 3 with the A and E, respectively. In measure 5 (IV) Leslie executes a classic B.B. King lick (repeated similarly in measures 10 and 11 for the IV and I chords) that has become one of his signature licks as well. Measures 7 and 8 (I) have the E composite blues scale around fret 5 (as do measures 9–12)

providing the 6th (C#), 5th (B), and major 3rd (G#) notes that resolve to the root (E) in measure 8. The same scale provides the root (B), 9th (C#), 4th (E), and 5th (F#) in measure 9 over the V chord (B). Be sure to observe the way Leslie uses the E note sustained on beat 3 of measures 9–12 as a motif or compositional device, with the harmony changing from the 4th over B (in measures 9 and 12) to the 5th over A (in measures 10 and 11), all of which creates exciting musical tension.

Performance Tip: For the "bendy licks" in measures 5, 10, and 11, push up the F# note on string 2 with your ring finger (backed up by your middle and index fingers) while accessing the B on string 1 with your pinky.

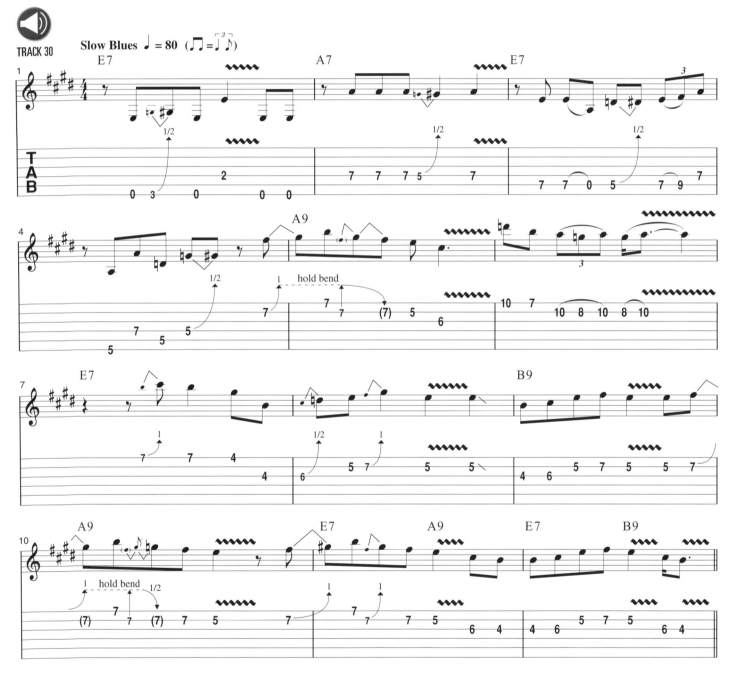

Leslie West Selected Discography

With Mountain:

Climbing! (Sony)

The Best of Mountain (Columbia)

Greatest Hits Live (King Biscuit)

GUITAR NOTATION LEGEND

Guitar Music can be notated three different ways: on a *musical staff*, in *tablature*, and in *rhythm slashes*.

RHYTHM SLASHES are written above the staff. Strum chords in the rhythm indicated. Use the chord diagrams found at the top of the first page of the transcription for the appropriate chord voicings. Round noteheads indicate single notes.

THE MUSICAL STAFF shows pitches and rhythms and is divided by bar lines into measures. Pitches are named after the first seven letters of the alphabet.

TABLATURE graphically represents the guitar fingerboard. Each horizontal line represents a string, and each number represents a fret.

4th string, 2nd fret · 1st & 2nd strings open, played together · open D chord

HALF-STEP BEND: Strike the note and bend up 1/2 step.

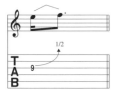

WHOLE-STEP BEND: Strike the note and bend up one step.

GRACE NOTE BEND: Strike the note and immediately bend up as indicated.

SLIGHT (MICROTONE) BEND: Strike the note and bend up 1/4 step.

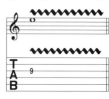

BEND AND RELEASE: Strike the note and bend up as indicated, then release back to the original note. Only the first note is struck.

PRE-BEND: Bend the note as indicated, then strike it.

VIBRATO: The string is vibrated by rapidly bending and releasing the note with the fretting hand.

WIDE VIBRATO: The pitch is varied to a greater degree by vibrating with the fretting hand.

HAMMER-ON: Strike the first (lower) note with one finger, then sound the higher note (on the same string) with another finger by fretting it without picking.

PULL-OFF: Place both fingers on the notes to be sounded. Strike the first note and without picking, pull the finger off to sound the second (lower) note.

LEGATO SLIDE: Strike the first note and then slide the same fret-hand finger up or down to the second note. The second note is not struck.

SHIFT SLIDE: Same as legato slide, except the second note is struck.

TRILL: Very rapidly alternate between the notes indicated by continuously hammering on and pulling off.

TAPPING: Hammer ("tap") the fret indicated with the pick-hand index or middle finger and pull off to the note fretted by the fret hand.

NATURAL HARMONIC: Strike the note while the fret-hand lightly touches the string directly over the fret indicated.

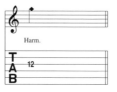

PINCH HARMONIC: The note is fretted normally and a harmonic is produced by adding the edge of the thumb or the tip of the index finger of the pick hand to the normal pick attack.

PICK SCRAPE: The edge of the pick is rubbed down (or up) the string, producing a scratchy sound.

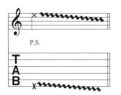

MUFFLED STRINGS: A percussive sound is produced by laying the fret hand across the string(s) without depressing, and striking them with the pick hand.

PALM MUTING: The note is partially muted by the pick hand lightly touching the string(s) just before the bridge.

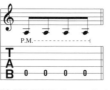

RAKE: Drag the pick across the strings indicated with a single motion.

TREMOLO PICKING: The note is picked as rapidly and continuously as possible.

VIBRATO BAR DIVE AND RETURN: The pitch of the note or chord is dropped a specified number of steps (in rhythm) then returned to the original pitch.

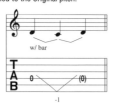

VIBRATO BAR SCOOP: Depress the bar just before striking the note, then quickly release the bar.

VIBRATO BAR DIP: Strike the note and then immediately drop a specified number of steps, then release back to the original pitch.